Registration Methods
for the Small Museum

ABOUT THE SERIES
The American Association for State and Local History Book Series addresses issues critical to the field of state and local history through interpretive, intellectual, scholarly, and educational texts. To submit a proposal or manuscript to the series, please request proposal guidelines from AASLH headquarters: AASLH Editorial Board, 2021 21st Ave. South, Suite 320, Nashville, Tennessee 37212. Telephone: (615) 320-3203. Website: www.aaslh.org.

ABOUT THE ORGANIZATION
The American Association for State and Local History (AASLH) is a national history membership association headquartered in Nashville, Tennessee. AASLH provides leadership and support for its members who preserve and interpret state and local history in order to make the past more meaningful to all Americans. AASLH members are leaders in preserving, researching, and interpreting traces of the American past to connect the people, thoughts, and events of yesterday with the creative memories and abiding concerns of people, communities, and our nation today. In addition to sponsorship of this book series, AASLH publishes *History News* magazine, a newsletter, technical leaflets and reports, and other materials; confers prizes and awards in recognition of outstanding achievement in the field; supports a broad education program and other activities designed to help members work more effectively; and advocates on behalf of the discipline of history. To join AASLH, go to www.aaslh.org or contact Membership Services, AASLH, 2021 21st Ave. South, Suite 320, Nashville, TN 37212.

Registration Methods for the Small Museum

Fifth Edition

DANIEL B. REIBEL

Revised by Deborah Rose Van Horn

ROWMAN & LITTLEFIELD
Lanham • Boulder • New York • London

Published by Rowman & Littlefield
A wholly owned subsidiary of The Rowman & Littlefield Publishing Group, Inc.
4501 Forbes Boulevard, Suite 200, Lanham, Maryland 20706
www.rowman.com

Unit A, Whitacre Mews, 26-34 Stannary Street, London SE11 4AB

Copyright © 2018 by Rowman & Littlefield
First edition 1977. Second edition 1984. Third edition 1997. Fourth edition 2008.

British Library Cataloguing in Publication Information Available

Library of Congress Cataloging-in-Publication Data Available

ISBN 9781442277113 (cloth : alk. paper)
ISBN 9781442277120 (pbk. : alk. paper)
ISBN 9781442277137 (electronic)

∞™ The paper used in this publication meets the minimum requirements of
American National Standard for Information Sciences—Permanence of Paper
for Printed Library Materials, ANSI/NISO Z39.48-1992.

Printed in the United States of America

Contents

Acknowledgments

This book is in memory of Daniel B. Reibel, curator, director, colleague, and, most important, teacher to many in the museum field. May this book help pass his wisdom on to the next generation of small museum collections staff.

To my husband, Lee, and my children, Elena and Alec, who were supportive and patient while I worked on this book.

Deborah Rose Van Horn

Introduction to the Fifth Edition

Registration Methods for the Small Museum was first published in 1977. At that time, Daniel Reibel planned on this book being a guide for volunteer staffs in the many small museums in the field. When the book was first published, a small museum was unlikely to have a paid staff. If it was lucky enough to have paid staff members, it is unlikely that they had training in handling museum records or collections.

The book was intended to be a guide for those managing the records and collections at small institutions, providing them with a reference tool when they did not know what to do. In the last thirty-nine years, we have seen the field professionalize, and many of these smaller institutions now have paid staff. This book has become a reference tool not only for the volunteers whom Reibel intended it for but also for countless museum studies students and museum professionals.

I was first introduced to this text when I entered the museum field as a graduate student in 1999. The conversational tone that Reibel used made this an easy text to read and learn about the career of a museum registrar. The simple explanations about paperwork, numbering systems, accessioning, and deaccessioning made the task of records management seem approachable.

The fifth edition of *Registration Methods for the Small Museum* will not be a complete rewrite of Daniel Reibel's work. Instead, I hope to let Mr. Riebel continue to teach the field through his own words while updating the text to reflect what is currently going on in the field. I hope that the next generation of museum volunteers, students and museum professionals will find this text as useful as I have through the years.

WHY A REGISTRATION SYSTEM?

What is a registration system, and why is it important? As Reibel said, "Your collection is not a museum until it has an adequate registration system."[1] A registration system is simply a system of record keeping to help track and care for the items in a museum collection. This book will define a registration system and give some examples of how these systems can be implemented in a small museum.

WHAT IS A SMALL MUSEUM?

It has always been difficult to define a small museum. Even different organizations in the field define a small museum in different ways. For example, the American Alliance of Museums defines a small museum as a museum with "fewer than five staff."[2] Meanwhile, the American Association for State and Local History defines the small museum as having an annual budget of less than $250,000, a small staff with multiple responsibilities, and the use of volunteers to perform key staff functions.[3]

The important thing is that the quality of your registration system should not be defined by the size of your staff or budget. In fact, small museums may have the advantage over larger institutions in the fact that they have smaller collections and it may be easier to get a handle on the records related to those items. Museum registration can be performed by a staff member or a volunteer. The important thing is to have some guidelines for the record keeping related to your collection so that there is consistency and information can be easily found.

INSIDE THIS BOOK

This book is intended as a guide to create a registration system for a small museum, so it is organized as a step-by-step manual to guide novices through the process. The content contains guidance for setting up the framework and includes discussions on governance, acquisition, numbering systems, accessioning, cataloging, loans, and deaccessioning.

Chapter 1: Why Have a Museum Registration System?

This chapter discusses the purpose and parameters of a museum registration system. It provides newcomers to the field with information on how to set up a mission statement and the scope of collections to help provide structure for the system. It also discusses why good documentation is so important.

Chapter 2: Acquisition

The acquisition chapter begins with a discussion of the different ways to gain title to objects in your collection. It discusses what documentation you need to obtain the title through donation, purchases, transfers, and so forth and discusses different ways to acknowledge a gift. The chapter concludes with information on what documentation needs to be the basis of the accession file.

Chapter 3: The Accession Number

This chapter discusses several different numbering systems that have been used in museums. The conversation looks at the benefits and problems with these different numbering systems so that the reader can decide which system will work best for his/her collection. The numbering information can also help the reader decipher old numbering systems in his/her collection.

Chapter 4: Accessioning

Now that the numbering system has been determined, the book will discuss how to accession the items into the collection. This chapter goes into a detailed discussion of how to create a record and what information should be captured for each object. The discussion includes information on how to number the items in the collection. It concludes with a look at deaccessioning museum collections.

Chapter 5: Documentation

This chapter looks at how museums document their collections through research, publication, and working with other groups and museums. The chapter includes a brief discussion on the differences between an accession file and a research file.

Chapter 6: The Catalog

Chapter 6 includes a discussion of the information needed to catalog an item in the collection. It discusses manual systems such as card catalogs and catalog books and briefly touches on computer catalogs. The conversation includes a look at classification systems such as nomenclature and authority lists.

Chapter 7: Loans

This chapter begins with a discussion on loan policies for museums and then moves on to the procedures that should be in place for a museum to lend items or accept them on loan from other institutions. The conversation includes the reasons for a loan and the things that should be included in a loan agreement.

Chapter 8: A World of Computers

Most registration systems are now in a database in a computer. This chapter looks at the things you should consider before purchasing or creating a collections management database. The discussion includes information on how to analyze what you need and then goes over the information you should be asking vendors before you purchase a system. The chapter also looks at topics such as fields in the database, security, storage, and backups.

CONCLUSION

I hope that you will find this edition to be as useful to your work in your institution as I have found it over the years. The technology we may use to do our job often changes but the basics of museum registration have remained the same through the years. This book is intended to be a guide to help in the registration process and make the job of caring for the museum collection easier. After completing this book, the reader will have a better understanding of the parts of a registration system and be able to use an existing system or create a new registration system for their institution.

I would like to thank Daniel Reibel for all of the guidance he gave me and many others through the years with the first four editions of this book. I hope that this fifth edition will help carry his legacy and lessons to the next generation of small museum caretakers.

Deborah Rose Van Horn

NOTES

1. Daniel B. Reibel, *Introduction of Registration Methods for the Small Museum*, 4th ed., 2.

2. http://www.aam-us.org/about-us/what-we-do/small-museums, accessed August 4, 2016.

3. http://community.aaslh.org/small-museum-what-is-a-small-museum/, accessed on August 4, 2016.

1

Why Have a Museum Registration System?

Most institutions do not have a corporate history that goes back beyond the memory of their most long-term employee. Tax records may have to go back as far as seven years, budgets may track three years, but most records seldom last much longer than a year. This is in marked contrast to museum collections records that theoretically last forever. The history of the object in the collection is an important component of it and is sometimes more important than the object itself.

The museum registration system is the museum's memory. Long after curators and registrars have come and gone, the records of the museum will speak. In keeping the historical story straight, they are as important as the object itself. A museum that fails to keep good records fails in its primary function—some would say its only function. With good records, more than the object is preserved. With poor records, something more valuable than the object may be lost.

The person, or persons, in charge of a museum have been given a trust. They have been placed in charge of a collection for a short period of time. It is their obligation and duty to see that the collection is well cared for and that it is passed on to the next caretakers in as good condition as when they received it. Good care includes good records. Good record keeping does not have to be difficult, time consuming, or costly.

There are collections of furniture, beer-bottle caps, art, matchbook covers, glass, ceramics, insulators stolen from telephone poles, seashells, animals, pornography, and so on. A museum may collect one or several of these things and more, but not all collections are museums.

As of 2016, the American Alliance of Museums had fourteen criteria for an accredited museum. Among those standards were the following criteria:

- be a legally organized nonprofit institution or part of a nonprofit organization or government entity.
- be essentially educational in nature.
- have a formally stated and approved mission.
- use and interpret objects and/or a site for the public presentation of regularly scheduled programs and exhibits.
- have a formal and appropriate program of documentation, care, and use of collections and/or objects.
- carry out the above functions primarily at a physical facility/site.
- have been open to the public for at least two years.
- be open to the public at least 1,000 hours a year.
- have accessioned 80 percent of its permanent collection.
- have at least one paid professional staff with museum knowledge and experience.
- have a full-time director to whom authority is delegated for day-to-day operations.

- have the financial resources sufficient to operate effectively.
- demonstrate it meets the Characteristics of Excellence for U.S. Museums.
- successfully completed the Core Documents Verification Program.[1]

Volunteer-run museums may not have a professional staff member but can meet all of the other criteria.

Private collections lack some of these characteristics. In 1990, the American Association of Museums defined a museum for accreditation purposes as "an organized and permanent nonprofit institution, essentially educational or aesthetic in purpose, with a professional staff, which owns and utilizes tangible objects, cares for them, and exhibits them to the public on some regular schedule."[2]

Notice the statement that the museum owns and cares for its collections. For accreditation purposes, care has been defined as protecting the essential integrity of the object and being able to account for it. The caring for collections is the essence of the difference between being a museum and not being a museum. The records are considered an important part of the object. Most museums that fail to be accredited fail because of the kind of care given to their collections. Many such failures come about because of the inadequate or incomplete records. A museum will be considered a good museum if the staff maintains good records but may not be considered a museum at all if that is not done.

The American Alliance of Museums has developed the Continuum of Excellence program to help museums strive for excellence and provide them with a roadmap to get accredited. In addition, they have developed a Small Museums Accreditation Academy to help small museums in this process. I would recommend visiting the American Alliance of Museums website for more information on these programs if you are interested in the current accreditation requirements or procedures.

Over the years, the museum field has developed a record-keeping system that is now pretty standard and consistent enough to be applied to the widely different circumstances of each museum collection. The system is actually quite simple. There is not much mystery to it, nor is there a need to invent your own record-keeping system.

HOW A HISTORY MUSEUM MAY DIFFER FROM OTHER KINDS OF MUSEUMS

There are differences between types of museums, and these are often reflected in their record-keeping procedures.

I must define the term "specimen" to make the rest of this discussion clearer. This term helps explain the difference among museums better than any other. It comes from a Latin root meaning "a distinguished mark," with the idea that the object stands out. Technically speaking, any object in a museum collection is a specimen. However, in the narrower use of the term, as often used in the museum field today, a specimen is an object that represents any other object in its class or type. It may be the best example, but it is still just representative. To some museums any specimen can easily be replaced by another, and better, one. Some museums separate their specimens from their collection, and even give their specimens a lower standard of care (think a hands-on collection). This concept of the object as a specimen is not universal in the museum field, nor even popular, but it is something to keep in mind.

The major difference between a history museum and other museums is that history museums collect objects that have some historical association attached to them. This historical association makes the object valuable all out of proportion to its value as a specimen or its monetary value. *It cannot be replaced by a better specimen.* Other characteristics of history museums are that the collection is of man-made objects, tends to be large, and is monetarily valuable. History museums share many of these characteristics with art and anthropology collections, but normally a history museum is the only type of museum where the major collecting effort is of objects with historical associations.

Registration systems in museums have to be flexible enough to account for these conditions and be able to record a lot of data on many objects.

Definitions

It is important to understand the terms used in this book, so I am listing some of them. My definitions are not exactly those of the dictionary, but they show the way these terms are commonly understood in the museum field today:

Accession: An accession is an object or a group of objects in the museum collection obtained at one time from a single source. The act of accessioning is taking possession and title to the object, placing it in the museum collection, and making a record of it.

Catalogue/Catalog: A catalogue (or catalog) is a reference tool created by arranging some of the collections records into categories.

Collection: A museum collection is a group of objects kept together for some reason. Usually the relationship is due to the similarities in the nature of the objects, their being collected by an individual or a group, or their association with a person, place, or event. A collection may have only a few pieces in it, or it may have thousands. A museum may contain one collection or several collections.

Collection Manager: This is a position often seen in larger museums whose purpose is the day-to-day care and maintenance of the collections in the museum. In smaller museums this function is often done by the registrar or the curator of collections. (See "registrar" below for more information.)

Curator: The definition of this term has been narrowed in the last few years, but for the purposes of this book the word means the professional person in charge of a collection. The collection may be a whole museum or only part of it. In some museums today, the curator may be responsible for research and someone else, such as the registrar or collections manager, is responsible for the collection.

Director: The person in charge of the museum. This term recognizes that the museum is not only its collections but also its program. The director is in charge of both administration and the museum's professional program.

Documentation: This is the factual information gleaned about each object in the collection. Some of this information is developed by examination of the object, and some is acquired by research. In some applications, the term "documentation" applies to all of the records in the registration system.

Museum: This is an institutionalized collection, the records of that collection, the physical plant where this collection is housed, and one that is potentially accreditable as a museum by the American Alliance of Museums.

Register: For our purposes, the register is a list of accessions, loans, and so on of the museum in some logical order.

Registrar: This is the person in charge of the museum's registration system. In the past few years the responsibilities of the registrar have been broadened to include extended responsibilities over the whole area of collection policy and management. In fact, the term "collections manager" is beginning to replace registrar in some museums as the preferred term. In museums without a registrar, the curator(s) or the professional staff is responsible for the records.[3]

Registration: This is the whole process of creating, acquiring, and keeping the records on a museum collection and is the subject of this book.

The person who is actually doing the registration should start with the attitude that registration is just one of the tasks to be performed so that some of the other tasks, such as acquiring more objects, preserving existing objects, and interpreting the collection, can be accomplished.

Boundaries

The Mission Statement

Policies have a way of affecting practices, and it is a good idea to make sure your policies are in order before developing practices. The first thing needed for a good registration system is a firm set of boundaries for the museum. This is found in the museum's statement of purpose and mission statement. These two are commonly combined into what is often called the mission statement. The mission statement should discuss what the museum is and what it is going to do.

Example
Hero County Historical Society

(purpose)
What Is the Museum?

The Hero County Historical Society is a nonprofit educational association.

And Its Purpose Is?

To collect, preserve and interpret the history of Hero County, Franklin.

For What Period of Time?

For the period of the arrival of the first Native Americans in this region until the present day, with special emphasis on the period since the founding of the county (1785) until the end of the nineteenth century (1900).

(mission)

By What Means?

By the collection of books, documents, artifacts, and other cultural objects, preserving them, and interpreting them to the public by means of a museum, educational programs, lectures, public events, and publications.

Any Other Qualifications?

To encourage others to collect, preserve, and interpret the history of Hero County and do everything worthwhile to carry out that purpose.

Written as a paragraph, the statement would look like this:

MISSION STATEMENT
Hero County Historical Society
   The Hero County Historical Society is a nonprofit educational association that collects, preserves, and interprets the history of Hero County, Franklin, for the period of the arrival of the first Native Americans in this region until present day, with special emphasis on the period since the founding of the county (1785) until the end of the nineteenth century (1900), by the collection of books, documents, artifacts, and other cultural objects, preserving them, and interpreting them to the public by means of a museum, educational programs, lectures, public events, and publications, and to encourage others to collect, preserve, and interpret the history of Hero County and do everything worthwhile to carry out our purpose.

This is a good mission statement because it confines the museum to the collection of only those objects related to the history of the county. Within that limit, it is very broad, as it allows the museum to collect almost everything. However, this statement is still a little wordy and can be narrowed down.

MISSION STATEMENT
Hero County Historical Society
   The Hero County Historical Society collects, preserves, and interprets the history of Hero County, Franklin, from the time of Native American arrival to the end of the nineteenth century. HCHS collects material culture documents and records to preserve and interpret them to the public through museum exhibitions, educational programming, and events.

This example still gives the museum boundaries but is much easier to remember. The mission statement should be reviewed periodically to make sure it is meeting the needs of the organization and accurately reflects the organization's mission. Often, museums review their mission statement whenever they revise their long-term plan—say, every five years.

THE COLLECTIONS MANAGEMENT POLICY

The collections management policy begins with the scope of collections, which defines what you collect and how you manage those collections. Often the scope of collections is a statement within a collections management policy, but some institutions prefer to have it as a stand-alone document. In this example, we will be treating them as one document, but the same questions and methodology can be used in developing the scope.

COLLECTIONS MANAGEMENT POLICY
HERO COUNTY HISTORICAL SOCIETY

What Type of Objects Will the Museum Collect?
   It is the policy of the Hero County Historical Society to collect only those objects made and/or used in Hero County, or are associated with a person, place, or event in the county, or, to a limited extent, are typical or representative of objects made or used in the county;

What Is the Scope of the Collection?
and that are historical, cultural, or aesthetic in nature;

Is There a Limit on the Period of the Collection?
that cover the period from 1785 to 1900;

Are There Any Other Limits?
and for which the museum has an ultimate use and for which the museum can care for under standards acceptable to the museum field at large.

Written out as a paragraph, this statement would look like this:

> COLLECTIONS MANAGEMENT POLICY
> HERO COUNTY HISTORICAL SOCIETY
> It is the policy of the Hero County Historical Society to collect only those objects made and/or used in Hero County, or are associated with a person, place, or event in the county, or, to a limited extent, are typical or representative of objects made or used in the county; that are historical, cultural, or aesthetic in nature; that cover the period from 1785 to 1900; and for which the museum has an ultimate use and for which the museum can care for under standards acceptable to the museum field at large.

This statement defines the collection a little more narrowly than the statement of purpose. The object should have a direct association with some person, place, or event in the county, but there is a clause allowing the museum to collect "representative" objects. The museum cannot collect seashells since they were not made or used in the county and are not historical, cultural, or aesthetic in nature. The museum cannot collect a locomotive, unless it will have some use for it and can take care of it. These conditions may not be too confining, and they will keep the museum's collection activities concentrated on what it really needs and can care for.[4] The enforcement of such a policy will help prevent problems with deaccessions later.

The collections management policy and the scope of collections keep the museum focused on what it is really trying to do. Before you develop any collection manual, you should make sure that your policies define a method of reaching your goals and that everyone understands them.

Collections Management Policy Manual

All the policies and procedures that affect the collection should be brought together in a collections management policy manual. The reason for having a manual is that there will be a consistent set of practices through several curatorial administrations. It is important that the manual reflect actual operating practices, be useable by anyone, and be short and easy to read. Collections management policies are not stagnant documents. They need to be reviewed regularly and updated when needed.

Even the smallest museum needs legal advice on exactly how the whole collections policy should be handled. It is a good idea to have the museum's whole collection policy looked over by a good lawyer.

The procedures carry out the policy and may require certain practices that affect policy. The manual should include both policies and procedures. The board should be involved in developing the manual and in carrying out its provisions. There are two sample collection management policies in the appendix.

What Does a Registration System Do?

After coming this far in the chapter I should at least explain what a museum registration system does. The registration system is a system of policies, procedures, practices, and documents that provides a link between the objects and their history and ensures that:

- The museum's right of ownership of the object is established.
- Associations with a person, place, or event are preserved.
- Interpretation of the object is enhanced.
- Preservation of the object is aided.
- The museum can identify and account for every object in the collection.

In order to do all these things, the museum muse have a well-developed collection policy and a set of procedures to carry it out.

The Rule and Its Test

There is a rule that should apply to any museum registration system. That rule is:

Any registration system used by a museum should be readily understandable to any intelligent but uninformed layman using the registration system itself, without any human assistance.

The museum does not need a high priest or priestess to interpret a divinely inspired registration system to the benighted masses below. What is needed is a system that anyone can understand in the event that the curator is not there to explain it.

The test of any system is:

- The museum should be able to produce any object from its collection from any document picked at random from its registration system.
- The museum should be able to produce all the documentation for any object picked at random from its collection.

If your museum cannot pass The Test, keep working on the problem until you can. I have seen some large museums with large professional staffs that cannot pass The Test and some small volunteer-run museums that can. The size of your institution does not determine the quality of your registration system!

Who is Responsible?

There is almost always a board or governing body responsible for the museum. That group has the ultimate responsibility for the collection. The board decides who is actually going to do the work.

In a museum with a professional staff, the decision is much easier: the professional staff does the work. The board has delegated its responsibility for the area of the museum to the professional staff, and those persons, among other things, are responsible for the records. It does not matter how large the staff is; if the curator or director is the only paid professional, that person is responsible. In situations where there is more than one professional, the director may delegate the responsibility. If the museum is fortunate enough to afford it, there will be a registrar, but do not get the chain of responsibility confused. The governing body is responsible and delegates its authority to the professional, who may further delegate it. If something goes wrong, it is the professional's responsibility. If the governing board allows the error to continue, it is its responsibility. With apologies to Lewis Carroll, what I have told you three times is true.

In the case of the volunteer-run museum, the governing board not only has the responsibility but also must do the work. In that event, there is usually a person or group of persons willing to undertake the care of the collections. This person or group assumes the functions of a curator and registrar. This office may be incorporated into a collections or museum committee. The committee takes charge of the registration system and reports to the governing body on its activities from time to time. These volunteer-run museums can have very effective records. Whether run by volunteers or professionals, a museum can have the kinds of records it wants. If the people involved in the museum are committed to a good registration system, they will have it, whether or not there is a professional on the staff. Unfortunately, the opposite corollary is also true.

The collections committee of the governing body offers an extra bit of continuity and responsibility to the collection, and can make the transition from one curator to another or from one administration to another, more easily than it would otherwise be. For these reasons, I feel that a museum should have some committee to oversee its collections regardless of whether the museum has a professional staff.[5]

First Steps

The ideal situation is not to have a previously registered collection at all so you can start from scratch. New organizations ae actually very fortunate in this respect. A new organization can develop a registrar's manual before it ever acquires a single object and can have an accurate and complete registration system from the beginning.

Museums that already have collections may not be so lucky. If your collection has been well cared for and you have good records, you are probably reading this book for the fun of it. If your collection has not been taken care of, and the records are a mess, you have a problem to solve before you do anything else (see figure 1.1).

Of course, there are also museums that fall in between the extremes of the new collection and the poorly documented collection. These museums have periods of good documentation and periods of bad or no documentation. This scenario can sometimes be the most frustrating because you often feel as though you are missing something.

If you are dealing with bad documentation or sporadically bad documentation, you will need to follow the same steps. Treat the collection as though all of the records are bad documentation.

Dealing with Bad Documentation

I would suggest that any museum starting with disorganized collections should start with a computer. The computer database is, after the initial start-up, easier, quicker, and a lot cheaper to use than any manual system. However, it also takes a lot of planning and a large commitment of time and resources on the part of the museum to carry out the job. (See chapter 8 on computers.)[6]

If your museum has a poorly cataloged collection, your first task is to get it into shape. It is difficult to tell someone how to do this without actually seeing the collection, but there are some things that can be done with any collection.

Assemble All the Records

The first task is to assemble all of the records you have and try to sort them out. Think of yourself as an auditor with a terrible bookkeeping system that has to be straightened out, particularly as the IRS is on its way. Start by sorting the records you have by year. Next, try to match any correspondence you find with objects listed in your files. If anyone was around when the mess was created, try to get them to advise you. Ask anyone who is familiar with the museum what they know about the collection. Look at old board minutes. Send an email or a letter to former staff members or volunteers who have moved. Just remember, the old system made some sense to someone at some time; try to figure out their reasoning, no matter how disorganized that may be, and you have won half the battle.

Make a Register

The written information must be in some usable form. I suggest making a register of old records by accession number (see figure 1.3). When you find an accession number, this will quickly lead you to the right data. If there are

FIGURE 1.1.

Ledgers and registers can come in many shapes and sizes. Be sure you check all documents, books, and so on in the collections areas to make sure you do not overlook something.

Photo by Deborah Rose Van Horn

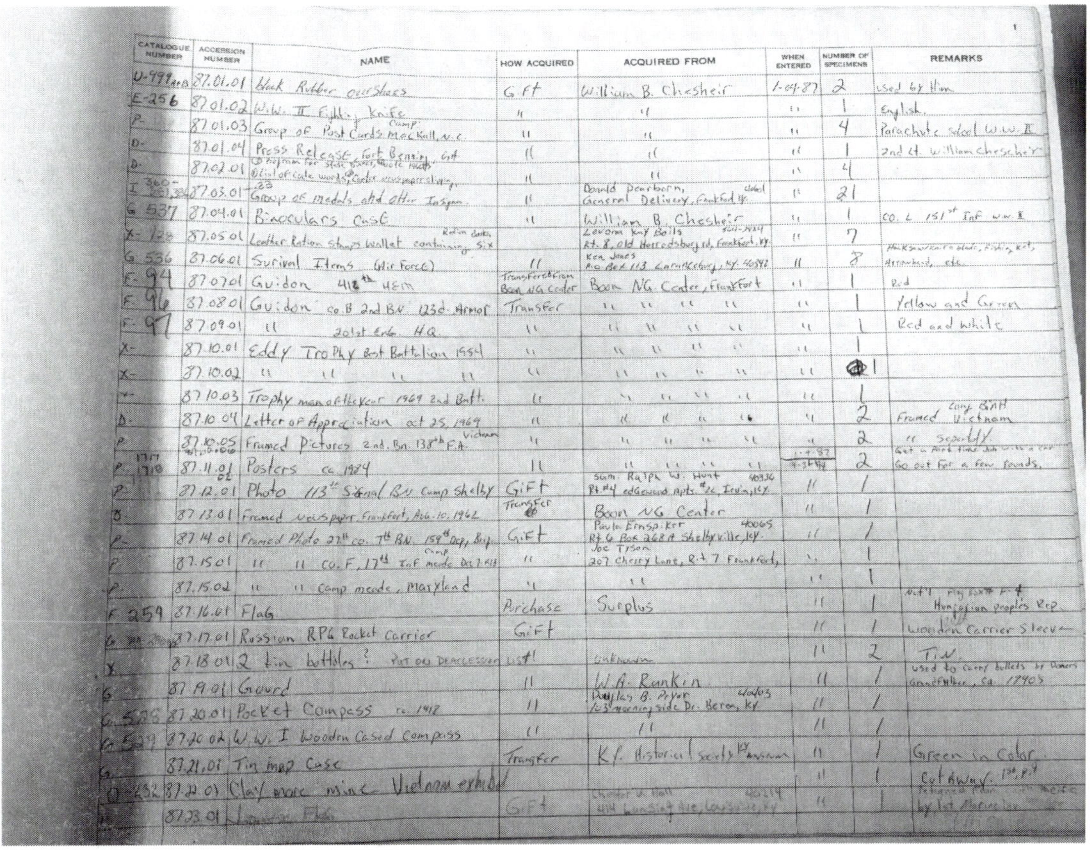

FIGURE 1.2.

This page is from a bound ledger kept until 1995. Most museums kept similar ledgers until after World War II. Whatever weaknesses this format has, it kept data in order (usually the order received).

Courtesy of the Kentucky Historical Society

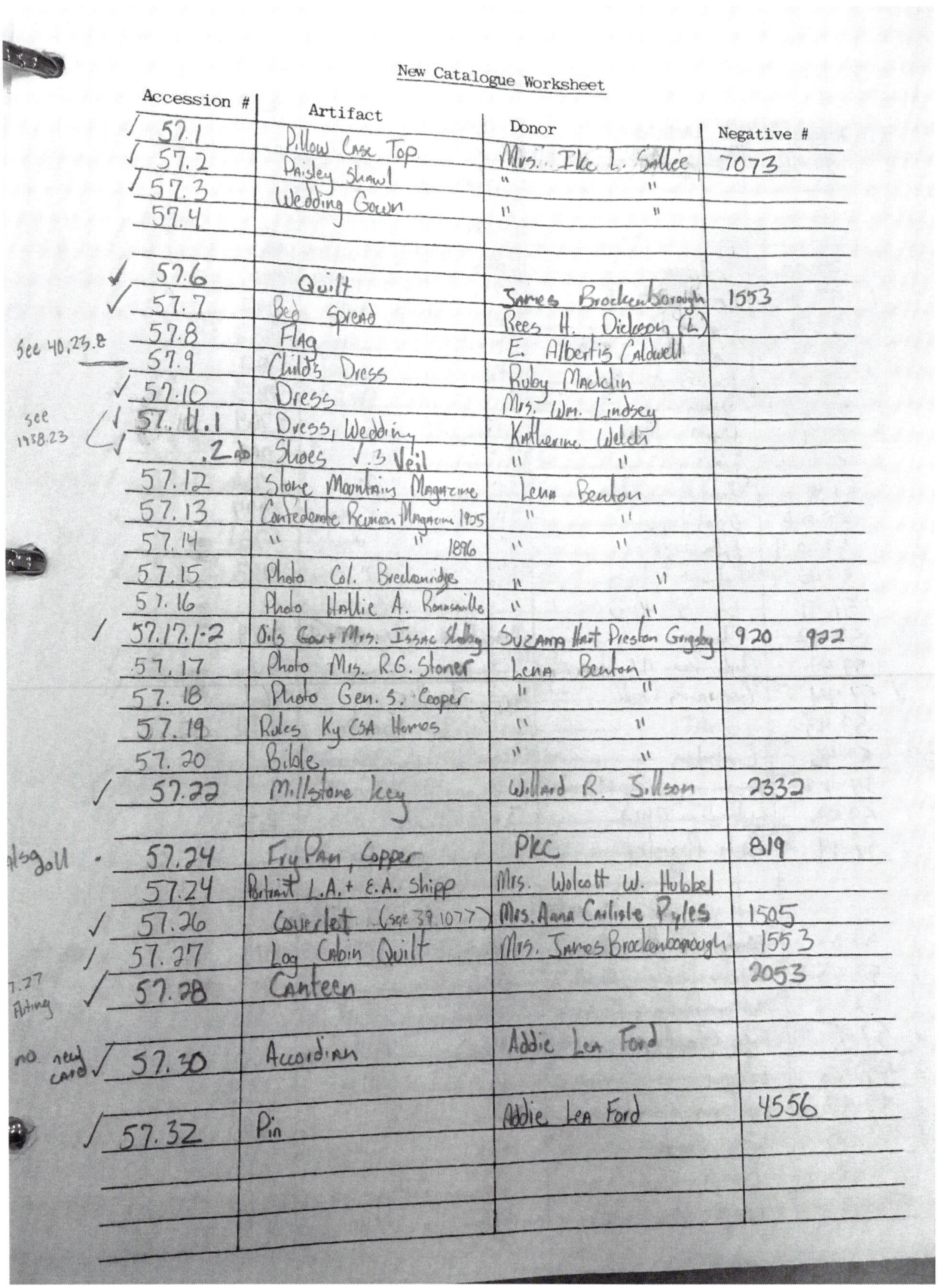

New Catalogue Worksheet

Accession #	Artifact	Donor	Negative #
✓ 57.1	Pillow Case Top	Mrs. Ike L. Sallee	7073
✓ 57.2	Paisley Shawl	" "	
✓ 57.3	Wedding Gown	" "	
57.4		" "	
✓ 57.6	Quilt	James Brockenborough	1553
✓ 57.7	Bed Spread	Rees H. Dickson (L)	
57.8	Flag	E. Albertis Caldwell	
57.9	Child's Dress	Ruby Macklin	
✓ 57.10	Dress	Mrs. Wm. Lindsey	
✓ 57.11.1	Dress, Wedding	Katherine Welch	
.2	Shoes ✓ .3 Veil	" "	
57.12	Stone Mountain Magazine	Lena Benton	
57.13	Confederate Reunion Magazine 1935	" "	
57.14	" " 1896	" "	
57.15	Photo Col. Breckenridge	" "	
57.16	Photo Hollie A. Ronasville	" "	
✓ 57.17.1-2	Oils Gov.+ Mrs. Issac Shelby	Suzana Hart Preston Grigsby	920 922
57.17	Photo Mrs. R.G. Stoner	Lena Benton	
57.18	Photo Gen. S. Cooper	" "	
57.19	Rules Ky CSA Homes	" "	
57.20	Bible	" "	
✓ 57.22	Millstone Key	Willard R. Sillson	2332
57.24	Fry Pan, Copper	PKC	819
57.24	Portrait L.A.+ E.A. Shipp	Mrs. Wolcott W. Hubbel	
✓ 57.26	Coverlet (see 39.1077)	Mrs. Anna Carlisle Pyles	1505
✓ 57.27	Log Cabin Quilt	Mrs. James Brockenborough	1553
✓ 57.28	Canteen		2053
✓ 57.30	Accordian	Addie Lea Ford	
✓ 57.32	Pin	Addie Lea Ford	4556

Side notes: See 40,23.8 ; see 1938.23 ; also doll ; 7.27 filming ; no new card

FIGURE 1.3.
Page from a register made prior to entering this data in computer data base. Notice the gap between numbers 57.30 and 57.32. This is common where no register was used.

catalog cards, you can organize them by the type of object. That will give you two ways to find something: either by number or by object type. This can then be applied to computer records to help index them into some useful form.

Don't Move Anything

Do not move any objects until you have their present locations firmly fixed in the records and in your mind. Objects are often left in one location in the museum for long periods of time, even decades. The relationship of the object to its location may be preserved in the records or the memory of someone associated with the museum.

Make an Inventory

It is a good idea to make an inventory of the museum before you move anything. Do one room at a time, making a short description of everything in the room. All objects found in the museum when the new registration system is set up should be noted. If objects have numbers, make a register of them. You can record locations through a video or through photography before you start the inventory.

A computer file is usually a lot easier to use than a card file. For example, you can search for all the tables forty-three to forty-six inches long and have a chance of finding the forty-five-inch table you are looking at. However, you may have to be inventive with your search parameters if the library table you are searching for has been mislabeled as a dining table. Inaccurate information can make searches more difficult, but the advantages often outweigh the disadvantages. For example, you can have the computer generate a catalog by number, title, and location if the information exists. This can be extremely useful in an inventory.

After you have fixed the location of each object, try to put the records for all of one type of object together. If you have all of the tables together, a description such as "one old table" may suddenly have meaning.

If the Collection Is Numbered

If the collection is numbered, try to reconcile those numbers with the collection records. The logic of the system will become clearer when you do this. I have found that, in these situations, the numbers on the objects usually have a reasonable relationship to the numbers in the records. I have found it easiest to make a register of the numbers from the records and check them off as I find the objects. That way I avoid duplications. You will also find numbered objects that have no apparent relationship to the records.

If a numbering system is completely disorganized, you may have to use a combination of techniques dealing with both numbered and unnumbered collections.

Do not assume just because the object is marked with an accession number that it has been accessioned. Conversely, if the object is not numbered, it may still have been accessioned.

If the Collection Is Not Numbered

If the collection is not numbered, you should assign numbers during the inventory. It is difficult to advise anyone on how this is to be done without seeing the collection records, but these rules apply to almost all situations. You should take steps to see that:

1. The fact that the objects are not numbered should be preserved in the numbering system.
   a. If the objects have a known status (i.e., a known provenance or source), you would assign numbers to objects in the same fashion that you would for any other accession.
   b. If the objects are of unknown provenance, then you accession them as one big group.

i. You can assign an artificial year of accession. If you are working in 2017, all the items of unknown provenance are accessioned as if in 2016. That is, any object numbered 2016.XX.XX is of unknown provenance. If the previous year has been used in your registration system, use system ii.

or

ii. You can assign an artificial donor or source number, perhaps a number 00 (double zero). With this system, if you are working in 2017, all the accession numbers 2017.00.XX are of unknown provenance. This is the method that I prefer to use instead of the artificial year.

2. You must keep an accurate register of what you have done.
3. You must place the accession number on each object as it is accessioned

How to Reconcile the Completed Catalog

You will end up with three classes of objects:

1. Objects that can be related to the records.
2. Objects that cannot be identified from the records.
3. Records that are not related to any object.

The tendency is to assume that unidentified objects do not have records and that the loose records refer to missing or stolen objects. Before these assumptions are made, carefully try to match the records with the objects. My experience has been that many of the objects thought to be "missing" actually exist in the collection, but the records are too disorganized to identify them. Some pretty strange descriptions creep into files. I have seen measurements off by as much as a foot, beds described as stands, cider presses described as lard presses, and so on. After you have carefully compared the records with the objects, you will have to admit that some discrepancies have crept into your records. These discrepancies can be "resolved" by reaccessioning the objects.

Never Throw Out Old Records

Never throw out old records, no matter how confused they are. Even if the records are completely disorganized, someone in the future may want some information from them. Never discard an old numbering system. Even if you renumber everything, you should carefully note the old numbers in the new records. The old numbers may be referred to in your registration documents.

If There Are No Records

If there are no records, you must treat the whole collection as a single accession. You can use the same techniques that you would in an unnumbered collection.

Be Complete and Consistent

The reason old registration methods may be a mess is often that whoever was keeping them was not consistent and did not complete what they set out to do. If you do not want someone to curse the day you were born, you must complete what you start, and you must be consistent. That means you must account for every object and reconcile all problems in the records. It is better to do one section of the old collection at a time, and do it well, than to try to do it all and be unable to complete what you start. Even if you are not using the most efficient procedures, your consistency and completeness will make the system useful.

Be Cautious about Reaccessioning

And finally, if you have a problem, reaccessioning is not always the way to solve it. You can end up with several registration systems. It is better to salvage the old system in order to preserve much of the original character of your records. A good way to salvage an old system is to catalog it. See chapter 6.

Make a Record of What You Have Done

Write down a description of what you have done, and make sure that this is preserved in your records. I would recommend binding it in the front of your accession ledger for the years you updated the records or making it an appendix for your procedural manual. Be sure to record any discoveries that you made about the old system.

What you are trying to do is make sure that those who come after you understand what you did and why. It is too much to expect someone to understand the basic logic of your actions without some explanation. I have seen dozens of collections where someone "renumbered" or "recataloged" it in some illogical and incomplete fashion, leaving no record of what they did or why, and creating a tremendous mess that causes problems for interminable periods of time afterward. If they had left a short explanation, it would have made things easier on the rest of us.

Volunteers and Registration

Museum professionals differ about using volunteers in general and using them in registration in particular. There is some negative feeling, and volunteers tend to be used mainly in the areas of interpretation and program. Volunteers can be very useful in the area of registration if the professional staff gives them some training and sets realistic, specific goals and works with them.

Collectors and knowledgeable people might be willing to catalog your collection in their area of interest. Bottle collectors might work with your bottle collection, stamp collectors with your stamps, gun collectors with your weapons, and so on. You can also find retirees with expertise in areas to help catalog with their knowledge. For example, I once had a retired surgeon assist me with identifying and cataloging the items in a collection of medical tools.

If you can tap that expertise, you can tap a whole community of interest that can help the museum with exhibits, publications, and collections and who can steer valuable information into your collection. The computer is ubiquitous in our society, and many people have sophisticated backgrounds in computers and data management. These people can give you real assistance.

I personally find volunteers to be very useful, their knowledge helpful, and their enthusiasm rewarding. I would not run a museum of any size without them.

Ethics

Morals Are Private, But Ethics Are Public

A legal friend once advised me never to do anything, no matter how innocent, that I would not mind discussing in open court. For ethics, that is a good rule to follow. Ethics codes usually urge people to avoid even the appearance of impropriety, and the museum collection is one area where that is a sound practice. The Accreditation Commission insists that all museums being accredited adopt an institutional code of ethics. Whether you intend to be accredited or not, it is a good idea to have one.

The museum field has evolved a consensus on ethics and has developed a number of ethics codes. The board ought to formulate such a code considering several factors discussed here.[7] A statement about ethics appears in the sample collection policies in the appendix.

It is not a good idea for the board member or the staff to be in the actual business of privately collecting, buying, and selling in the same area in which the museum's collection falls. These people in posts of trust or honor should avoid going into competition with the museum. People interested in the museum, and curators trained in its field of interest, will, as a matter of course, be knowledgeable about areas similar to that of the museum's collection and may privately own objects which could be in that collection. They may buy and sell from their own collection from time to time. They should inform the board if they have substantial holdings. If an object that should be in the museum's collection is offered to one of these persons, the person should offer the museum first refusal. If one of these privileged persons sells some of their own collection, they should offer it to the museum first. As a practical matter, the small museum will seldom be in a position to buy one of these objects, but knowledge of the transaction keeps everything visible so the board can be informed and make judgments wisely.

A knowledge of the marketplace is desirable in a curator. Many great collections have been built by a collaboration between a curator and dealers. However, it is undesirable for the curator or board member to operate an antiques shop or to be a partner, silent or otherwise, in one or to have a similar conflict of interests. I personally do not collect in the same area as the museum at which I work, but it is pertinent to remember that it may be desirable for other curators and board members to do so. If there is potential conflict, the board should set up a mechanism where everything is out in the open, so neither party is injured, but under which both can operate.

A colleague of mine once had to discuss the price she expected to pay for an object to be auctioned at a board meeting in front of a board member who was going to bid against the museum! You do not want to be in that situation.

CONCLUSION

The first steps, then, are important. The museum should decide that it is going to have a good registration system and set out to do what is necessary to achieve it.

- It is as important to know why you are doing something as it is to know how to do it.
- It is important to stay within definite boundaries.
- It is even more important to be consistent and to complete each process before going on to the next step.
- It is important to get all the information you can on each object and file it where it can be found.

That sounds like a lot to do, but the consequences of not doing it will take more time than doing everything on this list well.

NOTES

1. http://www.aam-us.org/resources/assessment-programs/accreditation/eligibility, accessed August 4, 2016.

2. *Museum Accreditation: A Handbook for the Institution* (Washington, DC: American Association of Museums, 1990), 26. An official of AAM pointed out to Reibel that this is for accreditation purposes only.

3. See Mary Case's *Registrars on Record* (1988), or Rebecca A. Buck and Jean Allman Gilmore's *Museum Registration Methods*, 5th ed. (2010), 2–13.

4. There are numerous discussions of collections policies and scopes of collections. See John E. Simmons, *Things Great and Small: Collections Management Policies* (Washington, DC: American Association of Museums, 2006), and Marie Malaro and Ildiko Pogany DeAngelis, ed., *A Legal Primer on Managing Museum Collections*, 3rd ed. (Washington, DC: Smithsonian Books, 2012). A useful outline of Ms. Malaro's ideas appears in "Collections Management Policies," in Anne Fahy, ed., *Collections Management*, Leicester Readers in Museum Studies (New York: Routledge, 1995), 11–28, with a sample collection policy; other volumes on the topic include Marilyn Phelan, *Museum Law*, 4th ed. (Lanham, MD: Rowman & Littlefield,

2014), and James B. Gardner and Elizabeth E. Merritt, *The AAM Guide to Collection Planning* (Washington, DC: American Association of Museums, 2004).

5. The use of a collection committee is not a standard practice in the history of the museum field, but, in my opinion, it should be. See especially Malaro, *Primer*.

6. This section modified from an address given by Daniel Reibel at a Mid-Atlantic Association of Museums meeting in Washington, DC, 1994; Rebecca A. Buck and Jean Allman Gilmore, *Collection Conundrums* (Washington, DC: American Association of Museums, 2007), 24–31.

7. Jackie Weisz, compiler, Roxana Adams, series editor, *Codes of Ethics and Practice of Interest to Museums* (Washington, DC: American Association of Museums, 2000); Rebecca Buck, "Ethics for Registrars and Collections Managers," and Ildiko Pogany DeAngelis, "Collections Ethics," in Buck and Gilmore, *Museum Registration Methods*, 394–99. The International Council of Museums' Code of Ethics can be accessed on its website. The quote about ethics being public was once a common saying in the museum field. I have not heard it lately, but it is true more often than not.

2

Acquisition

The first stage of the registration process is the acquisition of the object. This process starts with the first contact with the owner of the object. Someone may approach the museum with an item they wish to donate or sell, or the museum may approach them. Museums acquire objects mainly by two methods, as gifts or purchases. However, these are not the only ways that a museum may acquire an object. Methods of acquisition may include:

- Gifts/donations
- Purchases
- Exchange
- Bequests
- Transfers from another museum
- Collection in the field

Any documents created by this contact, particularly letters, bills of sale, and notes, become the first items in your accession file.[1]

ACQUIRING TITLE

The most important thing about these first steps in the registration process is that the museum gets actual title and possession of the object and a document proving that the museum owns it. You would be amazed at the number of museums that cannot prove that they own their collections. Title passes to you when you acquire all the rights of ownership—that is, the right to do anything that the museum wants to do to the object.

In order to pass good title to you, the person transferring the object must have good title themselves. They must have unrestricted rights to the object and be free to give or sell it to the museum. The museum should question the owner on that right. There is a considerable difference between acquiring an object that has been in a family for generations and buying it from some unknown dealer off the back of a truck. In the case of gifts, the museum should make sure that there is not some other person in the family with an interest in the object. You cannot acquire an object from a juvenile without parental permission, and even this may come into question when the juvenile reaches majority.

In gifts, the first steps that the museum takes should ensure that it acquires these rights:

- *The right to display or not display the object as the museum pleases.* If the museum is bound to display something permanently, that would bind them to one kind of exhibit forever.

- *The right to break up collections.* If the museum is given a collection of household objects, it might be expedient to store the glassware in one place and the ceramics in another, rather than keeping it all together. The museum may wish to keep the collection in a general ledger. The museum may wish to keep only part of a collection and dispose of the rest.
- *The right to dispose of the object as the museum sees fit.* Although the museum does not intend to dispose of any of its collection, there are times when it has too many of one thing and can trade or sell them and should not be restricted from doing so.

It is better to acquire all these rights at the beginning and not have to worry about them later.

These rights of property may sound harsh to a prospective donor, but the donors themselves would not want to own property with any restrictions on it, and neither does the museum. Contrary to what these rights imply, the museum is under a heavy responsibility to keep everything it acquires. Museums that "churn" their collections inevitably get into trouble.[2]

Copyrights and Trademarks

Keep in mind that certain rights may not belong to the owner. The most ordinary ones would be copyright or trademark. You can pretty much assume that if a copyright is not specifically transferred to you in writing, you do not own it. The law on copyrights is very complex.[3] Copyright notices do not have to be placed on objects after January 1, 1978. Trademarks expire periodically, but some are kept alive long after the original company that owned them has gone out of business.[4]

Laws and Provenance

The legal world can be confusing when it comes to acquiring title to a piece. It is best to be familiar with any number of laws relating to what is or is not legal. The confusing thing is that a practice that may be legal at the time of acquisition may also be subject to a law later. It is best to pay attention to what is going on in the field and see if it may impact your collection.

The Native American Graves Protection and Repatriation Act (NAGPRA, 1990) affirms the right of Native Americans and Native Hawaiians to custody of their human remains, funerary and sacred objects, and objects of cultural patrimony *that are in the control of federal agencies and museums.* If you have such objects in your collection, you may be under an obligation to return them. If the object was collected on federal land or was from a protected grave site, NAGPRA may apply. You should be aware that any Native American object should have provenance with it that proves that it is not under NAGPRA.[5] You can never can acquire good title for stolen goods, so examine provenance carefully.

Just before and during World War II (1938–1945) the Nazis stole huge amounts of artwork and cultural items from individuals, museums, and governments. Very little of that has been returned, but that does not mean the original owners lost all their rights. Any work of art with a shaky provenance during the war years is suspect. There are laws and treaties related to the return of the artwork that was stolen.

Currently, there are several conflicts going on in the world where a large number of antiquities are being looted from museums and archaeological sites. It is a good idea to be familiar with the countries that have been impacted and the treaties related to the looted antiquities and artwork. That way you can question anything of suspicious origin. Before you even borrow, let alone buy, an object with a questionable provenance, you should check with police. The FBI has a large division that does nothing but track stolen art.

Other laws that may impact clear title to a piece may deal with the materials that the piece is made from. There are laws related to items made from ivory, eagle feathers, and other materials that may have come from endangered species. You may also have questionable provenance if a piece was recovered from an abandoned shipwreck or taken from a national park.

It is best to find out as much as you can about the item and its history up front. That way there are no surprises. As an example, it is one thing to establish a good provenance for an item that has been in a family for generations and which may not have a single piece of paper as evidence. It is another question when a similar piece has no information that comes with it and the donor/seller cannot tell you who owned it before them.

PURCHASES

It is simpler to acquire the necessary rights with things you buy but not so simple with gifts. When a museum purchases something, it gets a bill of sale. If there is a willing seller who has unobstructed title to the object, a willing buyer, an exchange of equal value, and all the other processes of the marketplace, then you almost always have clear title to the object. The bill of sale and all other documents of the transaction should be marked with the accession number of the object and placed in the accession file.[6]

Even the smallest museum needs legal advice on exactly how such purchases should be handled. It is a good idea to have the museum's whole collection policy looked over by a good lawyer.

GIFTS

Most museums of any size depend on gifts of objects to make up their collections. When someone gives an object to the museum and the transaction is without value received, but only for goodwill, the museum's title to the object is not as clear as it is for a purchase. A gift normally passes absolute ownership from the givers to the recipients only when there is the intention to make the gift and free will on the part of the givers, something they, or their heirs, can deny later.

To help establish their title to gifts, museums should have donors sign a "transfer-of-title form" or "gift agreement form."[7] The gift agreement is pretty clear evidence of free will and intention to make a gift.[8] The actual owner will seldom, if ever, claim his or her property back. I have never had it done to me in fifty years in the museum business, although I know of cases where it has happened at other museums. In these cases, incidentally, the museums refused to return the objects and were upheld. Never, ever accept a gift without a properly executed gift agreement form. In the absence of any preliminary documents, such as temporary custody agreements, that will be the first document in the museum's accession file on that particular accession. Such a form should clearly state that the donor is giving up all rights and title to the object. A statement on such a document might be:

> I/We _____ hereby give to the trustees of the XYZ Museum absolute and unconditional ownership of the following, together with all copyright (in all media by any means now known or hereafter invented) and any associated rights which I/we have.[9]

The transfer of title should clearly state what is being given, show the date of the transaction, and provide a place for signatures of the donor and a representative of the museum. In some states you may need a witness to the signature. With this statement, the description of the property, and all the signatures, you have good claim to the object, but the title may not be absolute, and the watchful museum professional keeps that in mind.

A gift of an object to a history museum collection places an obligation on the museum. This obligation is to preserve the object and to keep all historic associations. Although these obligations are seldom mentioned, or placed in writing, they are usually assumed by the donor: "You're a museum, after all." Donors and communities become very upset when the museum does not live up to these expectations. There are several court cases where museums have been held remiss for failing to perform these unwritten obligations. That places a heavier load on gifts than on purchases, though this rule applies to the whole collection.

If the donor gives you money to buy something, the object purchased is a gift. You still have to get a bill of sale or a receipt for the purchase, but the accession is still a gift. Because the donor gave you money, the object is much more clearly the property of the museum than the gift of the object itself might be, but objects purchased in this way should be treated as any other gift. Since you already have a document transferring the object, you may not need a gift agreement form in these cases, but should have some sort of document from the donor indicating the gift.

With bequests to the museum, the executor or the lawyer handling the estate will usually supply some document, such as a copy of a portion of the will, or something similar. In many cases they will produce only a letter stating that he is executing the will and has the power to transfer the property to the museum. These documents are usually sufficient to establish title to the object, and you will not need a gift agreement signed, but every time this comes up check with your lawyers.

Occasionally you will be bequeathed items with restrictions on them. These restrictions might include the way the bequest is to be acknowledged ("In Memory of B. Knott Forgotten") but also might include the donation of objects you do not want or restrictions on the bequest, such as requiring that it be kept together in a collection or permanently exhibited. Each instance must be handled individually, but the institution must be careful not to place itself in the position of not being able to break up collections or always having to exhibit some particular object. You are not in a position to negotiate with the donor. If you accept the item as a bequest, you may have to keep it permanently, unlike other portions of your collections. In these cases, your lawyer can advise you.

Sometimes heirs to an estate will give items in memory of the deceased. These are not bequests from the estate, but are gifts from the heirs, and have to be treated like any other gift.

Museums also acquire objects by law. This is when objects are turned over to the museum in the normal legislative process. This most often happens when the museum is a government agency such as a state, county, or city museum, but it can happen in other types of museums as well. One is surplus goods from a government unit. Another example would be the Hero County Civil War battle flags being turned over to the Hero County Historical Society by action of the county commissioners. Some objects, such as archives, may be turned over automatically by law. It would be a good idea—mandatory, as a matter of fact—to get a signed letter of transmittal for such a gift. A receipt may be good enough here, but you can never get enough legal advice, so ask your lawyer.

Another means of acquisition is "field collections" or "collections in the field." This term usually applies to archaeological and scientific collections, but history museums also acquire objects in this fashion. Salvaging something from a junk pile might be the closest analogy to scientific field collection. If you get to salvage machinery from a factory that is to be torn down, that, too, is collection in the field. You should have some document showing you had the right to do this and that the items collected are yours. Collections in the field are handled as any other accession.

Museums exchange objects with other museums and institutions or give and receive transfers of objects. These deals are usually done on a friendly basis, but, again, you should have a document showing you have title. In the absence of any other document, the transfer-of-title form should be sufficient documentation. Usually each museum will send copies of its accession file with the exchange. Transfers and exchanges are handled as any other accession or deaccession.

It is not a good idea to accept an object on loan pending its donation as a gift. Some flexibility may have to be exercised here, as the museum may wish to examine it before accepting it, or the authorizing person may not be available. There is a method of doing this which is often called by the clumsy "deposit loan" or "temporary custody agreement." A deposit loan is a short-term loan (usually less than thirty days) that the museum takes in under much lower standards of care than other loans. The museum usually does not agree to any responsibility, other than to guard against gross negligence, and places all the responsibility for the delivery and pickup on the lender. These loans have to be tracked very carefully and cleared as early as possible. Deposit loans are discussed further in chapter 7.

POSSESSION OF THE OBJECT

Warning flags should go up whenever the owner does not want to give possession. Title to the object and possession of it are two different things in law, but, for practical purposes, you may assume that you do not have title unless you also have possession. In the case of gifts, title passes only with possession, particularly when there is a tax consideration. It would be difficult to imagine a valid purchase without the museum acquiring possession. There are, however, occasionally situations where possession of the object does not immediately pass to the museum. These deals should not be consummated without the advice of a lawyer and a discussion with the board.

There are "partial" gifts where the museum shares ownership with another person or museum. In these cases the museum owns only a certain percentage of the object and has possession only a portion of the time. Partial gifts are very difficult to handle. The number of potential problems is infinite. To have a partial gift in storage is ridiculous, and I would recommend not accepting partial gifts unless it is an object that you just have to have and that will add significantly to your exhibits.

There are gifts for which the owner may retain certain rights. An example would be a famous person retaining the right of publication to his or her papers. This is something to approach carefully, but if you must accept something with this kind of restriction, put a time limit on it—ten to twenty-five years is reasonable, or perhaps terminating on the donor's death.

A museum has to be careful about giving "life tenure" or long-term possession to the donor on objects in the collection. This is particularly true when a tax deduction is involved. The donor usually cannot claim tax deductions unless the title to the property has been transferred and the object itself is in the possession of the museum. You may have trouble getting such property away from the heirs. Museums are usually not in a position to engage in long and expensive lawsuits. The original owner seems to live forever.

At this point, whether it was a purchase or a gift, the object is now in the possession of the museum, and you have title to it. If you do not, go back to Go and start again.

ACKNOWLEDGMENT OF GIFTS

It is an excellent idea to acknowledge all gifts, both privately and publicly. There are several ways to do this. Many organizations have a printed form which they send to the donor to acknowledge the gift. That is adequate, but I prefer a personal letter. A gift is a declaration of faith in the museum and deserves more than a form letter. It takes very little effort to make each one personal. (See textbox 2.1.)

The person who receives this letter will know you really appreciated the gift. Notice the accession number on the lower left. A copy of this letter and of Mrs. Donor's letter of inquiry asking the museum if it wants the collection are placed in the accession file. The letter of inquiry can come in many formats, including a typed or handwritten note or an email. If the item is brought into the museum as a walk-in donation, this may even be a receipt that the donor signed indicating that they are leaving the piece with you to consider for acquisition. These documents, along with the public display of the objects as gifts, may prove a museum's claim to title in the future if the heirs should claim that auntie didn't know what she was doing when she gave away the spoons.

THE HERO COUNTY HISTORICAL SOCIETY

The John A. Hero Mansion

804 East Lincoln Avenue

Hero, Franklin 20123

July 6, 2008

Mr. B. Generous Donor

26339 York Road

Hero, Franklin 21123

Dear Mr. Donor:

I wish to thank you for the generous gift of the one-wheeled automobile. The museum depends on the generosity of donors to develop our collection, and we appreciate the trust you have placed in the museum by making this donation. It is an important addition to the collection and will be enjoyed by our visitors for years to come. You can see it on display in the Carriage House.

Please sign the enclosed gift agreement form and return it to us in the enclosed envelope. This form is the legal transfer of ownership and is the last step in completing your donation.

I wish to thank you for the gift on behalf of the Board of Trustees of the Hero County Historical Museum.

Sincerely,

P. Bismarck Adams, Director

A good place to acknowledge a gift publicly is in your newsletter. It will give good publicity among people most interested in the museum and will encourage them, too, to give. Another place is a new-acquisitions exhibit in some good corner of the museum. This will be seen by the casual visitor. (See figure 2.1.)

If the item is exhibited, the label should acknowledge it as "Gift of Mrs. Deductible Item" or, in the case of a fund, "Purchased by the Faith, Hope, and Charity Fund." This is important, and the donors, their family, and their friends will receive a great deal of satisfaction from seeing the name on the label. If the name is left off, the donor and potential donors may quite rightly think that you do not care. That name is public evidence that the object was a gift. Publication of gifts in your newsletter is also a public announcement of the gift. All this publicity of the object as a gift helps document the museum's claim to it. Courts have ruled that the public display of an object with the unchallenged statement that it is a gift is evidence of the donation.

Some donors don't want their name used publicly. The reasons for this are various but usually involve the donors not wanting the public to know that they owned such an object. They may fear becoming targets for thieves or ungrateful relatives, or they may not want their family name attached to an unpleasant historical event. You should

New in the Kentucky Historical Society collections

Bicycles, c. 1940

In another recent acquisition, the Kentucky Historical Society received two bicycles from the late 1930s and early 1940s. The first is a girl's Elgin safety bicycle used by Laverne Chesher Drane as a child in Louisville. The second bicycle is a boy's American Flyer "MotoBike." The American Flyer bicycle was used by Ollie Chesher Jr. as a child in Louisville. KHS museum purchase.

Tackle box that belonged to nationally recognized author and reporter Irvin Cobb. The tackle box will be displayed in the upcoming exhibit A River Runs Through Us: The Rivers of Kentucky.

Ollie Chesher Jr. and a friend ride American Flyer "MotoBike."

Irvin Cobb's Tackle Box

The Kentucky Historical Society is excited to add the tackle box of writer, reporter, and actor Irvin Cobb to its museum collections. Cobb was a nationally rec-ognized author from Paducah, Kentucky, who spent his career writing for several notable publications in-cluding, the *Saturday Evening Post* and *Hearst's International* and *Cosmopolitan Magazine*. Cobb also pub-lished over three hundred short stories and approxi-mately seventy books, including his most popular work, *Speaking of Operations*. In addition, Cobb was an avid fisherman and often praised the products of the Heddon Company. The Heddon Company named a bait rod and a fly rod lure after Cobb, call-ing the products, *Irvin Cobb's Choice*. KHS museum purchase.

Calk Family Medicine Chest

This wooden medicine chest and its contents were used by the Calk family of Mt. Sterling from the mid-1800s through the early 1900s. The chest has a hinged lid that opens to reveal a sectioned compartment de-signed to fit the medicine bottles the chest contains. A drawer at the front of the chest also opens to reveal

The Calk family medicine chest features a variety of at-home medical supplies dating from 1830 to 1930.

various medical instruments, including lancets for bloodletting, hypodermic needles, and an apothecary spatula. Many of the bottles within the chest were handblown glass and date to approximately 1830, but these bottles appear to have been reused or substi-tuted with modern medicine bottles as the family continued to use the chest. The latest bottle in the chest dates to approximately 1930. This medicine chest is an interesting look into the at-home medical practices of a Kentucky family through several gen-erations. Donated by Helene Perkins, Sharon Nesmith, Patricia Waggener, and Caswell Lane.

Fairchild Aerial Photographs, 1951

This collection of low-altitude, oblique views was created by Fairchild Aerial Surveys, Inc. of New York in 1951. The founder of the company, Sherman Mills Fairchild, was a pioneer in the field of aerial photog-raphy. His father was George Winthrop Fairchild, who served as a congressman from New York, and estab-lished a time-clock and adding-machine business that eventually became the International Business Ma-chines Corporation (IBM). In 1916, Sherman Fairchild developed the first synchronized camera shutter and flash. During World War I, he created a specialized camera with a large, between-the-lens shut-ter for aerial photography. By 1924, he established Fairchild Aerial Surveys Inc. and eventually began manufacturing his own planes as well.

This collection of ninety-one high-quality nega-tives focuses on industries in Louisville, Owensboro, Paducah, and the Kentucky Dam area in 1951. The collection features views of twenty companies, includ-ing B.F. Goodrich Chemical Co. and Tube Turns in Louisville, Fleischmann's Distillery in Owensboro, and Pittsburgh Metallurgical Co. in Calvert City. Transferred by The New Jersey State Archives.

—Deborah A. Rose

There is an easy way to make a gift to the Kentucky Historical Society

Have you been planning to send a check to An-nual Giving or thought about buying a personal-ized brick or leaf or an item in the Cradle-Day Gar-den, but never seem to get around to completing the form, writing the check, inserting everything in an envelope, and then actually *mailing* it? As time passes, do you kick yourself for not doing it?

Well, fret no more! The KHS Development Of-fice is here to help. Simply call (502) 564-1792, extension 4479. Tell us what you would like to do, and, presto (almost), it will be done! All you need to provide to make this happen is the desire and a valid MasterCard, VISA, Discover, or American Express credit card.

If you order a brick or leaf or any other com-memorative item, it would be helpful to plan your desired inscription before making the call. When you're stumped on how to fit that too-long inscrip-tion into the available space, we can also help with that. The folks in the Development Office have dealt with nearly 2,000 brick, leaf, and garden-bench inscriptions! You may also place your brick or leaf order via the Internet through the Society's Web site at www.history.ky.gov.

Once we process your gift, we will mail you a formal acknowledgement letter along with a copy of your charge slip.

Please be sure to let us know how you think we could make the overall giving/ordering process easier for you, our donors. We at KHS may be de-voted to Kentucky's history, but our customer-ser-vice methods are designed for the present.

8

FIGURE 2.1.

This is an acknowledgment page from a newsletter. This is a great way of acknowledging donors and making a public record of the donation. Kentucky Historical Society, Chronicle, 2003.

Courtesy of the Kentucky Historical Society

honor this request when asked. Privacy laws limit the publication of a donor's name to legitimate museum functions such as exhibits or publication of catalogs.

BOARD ACTION

The board of trustees has the ultimate responsibility for the museum. When the museum accepts an object for its collection it is also accepting a rather heavy long-term responsibility, and that makes it a board matter. The board should have knowledge, if not actual approval, of the acceptance of each object. That does not necessarily mean that every object has to be taken before the board and discussed. That would tie the board up with the minutiae that are best left to the professional staff. The easy way is to have the director take a list of accessions before the collections committee. Once approved, this can be submitted with the committee's report. By accepting the report, the board approves of the accession. This action will give the board necessary oversight without creating undue interference.

On accepting a gift, it should be made clear to the donor that the museum does not expect any problems with the acceptance; in fact, it is wise to mention in passing that the committee must approve. If the museum does not want the object, this provision allows it to turn down an object gracefully and spread the blame over the anonymity of a number of people. The acceptance of the collections report should be a routine thing, similar to the secretary's reading of the minutes. The report keeps the board members informed, gives them some oversight over the collection, and reminds them of their responsibility.[10]

PROPERTIES ARE NOT COLLECTIONS

Properties are expendable portable physical assets of the museum, such as desks, chairs, vacuum cleaners, lawn mowers, and so forth. These are items that will eventually wear out and have to be discarded. Properties are more of a problem for an accountant than a curator. The museum should state in the collection policy that the properties are not collections and should not be accessioned and that collection items should not be used as properties.

Many museums use reproductions of objects in their exhibits or for educational programs. These reproductions are properties and should not be treated as collections even though you may keep them separate from the other properties. In particular, they should not be accessioned.

If a reproduction is made by a well-known craftsman, it may have a high aesthetic, monetary, or cultural value. These objects might be the best in the collection. This is a quandary, for if it is in the collection, it should not be used in programs. We are going to discuss a tiered collection, where each tier receives different treatment, and that is one solution to the problem of valuable properties, if the museum can monitor it.

THE ACCESSION FILE

At this point you have a group of documents associated with the collection. These should be assembled into an accession file. Some museums have a separate file folder on each accession, some have a file on each object, and some have one for the year. The kind you will use will depend on the number of documents you have and your ability to store them. In any case, the accession number should be written in soft (#2) pencil on each document, if it does not appear as part of the document itself, so that it is associated with the object. An accession file will continue to grow as letters and other documents come in, years after the file is set up. This is the permanent record of the museum and should be in a fire-resistant file cabinet, if you can afford one. It is not a bad idea to scan the file periodically and store the information on a server. This provides you with a backup for the original file in case the original is damaged.

WHAT NOT TO DO AND WHEN NOT TO DO IT

I repeat myself here about several things that I have already recommended that should not be done when acquiring an object. Once more with feeling:

- Do not accept a gift without a transfer of title or buy an object without a bill of sale.
- Be very careful about accepting a gift that has any restrictions on it.

A major mistake a museum can make in the acquisition process is to put a valuation on the object for tax purposes. It is considered unethical to "buy" a donation with a high or inflated evaluation. It is illegal, too.[11] The museum can protect itself by making it a part of the collection policy or registrar's manual not to make evaluations. *It is the donor's responsibility to get a correct value for the gift for tax purposes.* You should be more than willing to cooperate with the donor on getting a professional evaluation and by making the object available to the appraiser if necessary. As part of the gift, the donor may want the museum to pay the appraiser. This is the same, actually, as the museum making the appraisal, and it should not be done. You may lose an occasional object by refusing to do this, but you will keep your integrity.

However, value is often part of the description. You may have two china plates, one of them worth five hundred dollars and the other fifty cents. Another example would be an object associated with a famous person. The association gives it a value beyond its value as an artifact. An example might be a Civil War uniform. If worn by an anonymous soldier from an unknown locality, it is a specimen. If worn by a local soldier whose history is known, then it is a valuable artifact. If you insure your collection, you will usually have to place a value on each object in the collection. This is the "book" value. The book value should equal "fair market" value. The value should not be public information.

TO REVIEW

The first step in the registration process is the acquisition of the object. The museum must make sure that it actually acquires title to the object, that there are no restriction on the museum's use of the object, and that all information about the object is recorded.

NOTES

1. There is extensive discussion of the acquisition process in Clarisse Carnell and Rebecca Buck's "Acquisitions and Accessioning" in *Museum Registration Methods*, 5th ed. (Washington, DC: American Association of Museums, 2010), 38–43.

2. "Churning" consists of acquiring and disposing of objects rapidly.

3. Copyright law is always evolving. New rulings may change what you can or cannot do with the copyright for an item. If you are unsure about whether you own the copyright or if you can use the item under "fair use," you should consult an attorney familiar with copyright law.

4. Michael S. Shapiro, Brett L. Miller, Christine Steiner and Nicholas D. Ward, ed., *Copyright in Museum Collections* (Washington, DC: American Association of Museums, 1999); Christine Steiner's "Copyright" in Buck and Gilmore, *Museum Registration Methods*, 5th ed., 427–36; Phelan, *Museum Law*, 313–50; Malaro and DeAngelis, *Primer*, 150–212. Malaro and DeAngelis also discuss other rights that may, or may not, come with the object.

5. Timothy C. Keown, Amanda Murphy, and Jennifer Schansberg, "Ethical and Legal Issues: Complying with NAGPRA," in Buck and Gilmore, *Museum Registration Methods*, 5th ed., 448–57.

6. Malaro, *Primer*, 234–47; Phelan, *Museum Law*, 202–15.

7. This may also be referred to as the deed of gift form or the certificate of gift form.

8. Phelan, *Museum Law*, 219–22 and Malaro, *Primer*, 234–47.

9. Malaro, *Primer*, 240–42. She also shows other forms mostly with much longer gift clauses.

10. Malaro, *Primer*, 14–17.

11. Phelan, *Museum Law*, 106, says that it performing a valuation runs against the ICOM *Code of Ethics for Museums* and may be seen as self-dealing for tax-purposes under federal law, 171–74. Malaro, *Primer*, 420–43, says it is a bad practice and has advice for avoiding the practice as well as handling referrals to outside appraisers.

3

The Accession Number

Curators and registrars are fascinated by the accession number. They spend a great deal of time with the numbering system. Numbers are almost a mystical kind of thing but they are fairly simple when you look at them. The number system gives a unique identity to each object. That number is used to tie the records to the object. If your system assigns a unique number to each object, then you have cracked the first layer of the mysteries of numbering.[1]

The rule in developing number systems is the one used in computer programs—"KISS." Keep it simple, stupid! There are four kinds of numbers to consider:

- *Serial number:* This number is one in a series, usually beginning at one, and taking each number in sequence. Letters may be a part of the system. All accession numbering systems in use today have a serial number as part of the accession number. Compare the "single-number system" and the "two-number system" below. They both are serial numbers.
- *Part number:* In this application, the number tells you something about the number as well as registering it with a unique number. The "three-number system" and its variations are part numbers, but they are also serial numbers.
- *Classification number:* This number is a kind of part number that indicates that the object belongs to a certain class of objects. Libraries use them, but a museum accession is usually not a book. Classification numbers work very well in libraries but not in museums. I do not recommend having a classification of the collection by number. I do not discuss them in this book.
- *Catalog number:* Explanations of a catalog number are always fairly vague. I have never had the need for it coherently explained to me. I will not discuss catalog numbers in any detail in this book. I do not recommend having a catalog number as separate from the accession number. The accession number can be considered a catalog number. There is often confusion between what is a classification number and what is a catalog number.[2]

The difference, if any, between an accession number and a registration number is discussed below. Let us look at how these different kinds of numbers are applied.

THE SINGLE-NUMBER SYSTEM

The easiest system to use is one with a single whole number for each object. The first object is numbered "1" (one), the second "2" (two), *seriatim*. The 912th object would be "912" and the 10,398th would be "10398." Nothing can be simpler than this! In fact, its logical construction and its very simplicity caused it to be used by the early museums in their first attempts to register objects. The Smithsonian Institution and National Park Service use a modified version of this system to this day. Although the single-number system went out of style in the 1950s and has been replaced, the increasing use of computers for museum registration has caused some people to reevaluate the system.

A single-number system can be made to function as a part number if you pair it with another field, such as the name of the object. Using the name and the number together creates a part number. In fact, you will seldom, if ever, see the accession number alone, without any other field.

The single-number system has a lot going for it. The single-number system has no complications. It is easy to understand and explain. One does not have to make decisions but simply takes the next available number. This may be important in small museums with inexperienced or untrained staffs and, perhaps, periods with no staff. It also gives you the finite size of the collection.

There are also some problems with the single-number system. If you get three accessions at once, one of which has two objects, another eight, and the third thirty-two, you have to complete the first accession before going on to the next one. This is because your system is strictly sequential and does not easily allow for entering one object of an accession now and another later. If you tried to allow for this by assigning eight digits to the second accession and then went to the third accession, you would have a problem if you suddenly discovered that there were actually nine objects, or only seven, in the second accession. The third accession of thirty-two objects may be much more important than the others, but you have to wait to do it until you have completed the other two because it is out of sequence. If the collection grows, the numbers may become very large. The donor of the objects is not identified in any particular way except as a block of numbers in a sequence. Museums account for their accessions by year, but there is no particular way to identify accessions by year except, again, as a block of numbers.

The other problem is that, depending on how your data management system sorts numbers, you may have to put "leading zeros" on each number. This is discussed in detail below.

There is nothing wrong with the single-number system, but for the reasons listed above, the single-number system has fallen out of favor with museums and has been replaced by other systems that I will discuss below.

THE TWO-NUMBER SYSTEM

To resolve some of the problems with the single-number system, museums have adopted a number that I will call the control number. The control is usually the year that the accession is made. If the year is 2016, then the control will be "016" for 2016. The second number is a catalog number. The first item registered would be 016.0, the second 016.2, the 394th would be 016.394, and so on. This system has some advantages. It divides the collections into blocks by year and makes accounting easier. It also stops the incessant sequence of one number following another and allows you to deal with groups of objects.

Some museums write this number as XX.016. It is not too important which method you use as long as you are consistent. However, listing the year first makes a long string of numbers more readable. If there is a standard in the method of numbering, it would be the year first.

The two-number system has solved the problem of always accessioning in the order received, but donors are not identified in any way by the numbering system.

One note about the control number or year in this system: Many older museums are dealing with more than one century of information. In these cases, it may be better to use the entire year instead of the abbreviation used above. (See section titled "How to Handle the Centuries" below.)

THE THREE-NUMBER SYSTEM

Because of these considerations, museums have developed what I will call the three-number system (sometimes called the "trinomial system"). In this system the second number is a source number, and there is a third number that I will call the catalog number. The source number is added into the two-number system.

In the three-number system, the first number, or control number, is usually the year of accession. The second number is the source number, and the third is the accession or catalog number. In this example, 016.23.14, "016" represents the year the accession was made (2016); "23" represents the twenty-third accession made in this year; and the "14" represents the fourteenth object in that particular accession. That is, there were thirteen objects registered before this one in the same accession. All objects numbered 016.23.XX come from the same donor at the same time.

This number may also be written in other ways depending on the system that was used. Other examples include:

2016.23.14   14.23.016   or   23.016.14

It strikes me that people who have systems using one of the last two examples are just trying to be different. The numbers in the last two examples will not line up on a page as well as they will when the year is placed first. That may be the reason that most museums place the year first, the control second, and the catalog number third.

The main advantages of the three-number system are, first, you do not have to worry about how many objects there are in each accession. The system can take care of any number. I once had over 3,100 objects in one accession. One does not have to take the accessions in sequential order, although you do have to complete them all before the end of the year.

The second advantage, and perhaps the most important, is that it identifies the donor or source of the accession by number. In fact, as we shall see, the three-number system can convey a lot of information, depending on how it is structured.

The three-number system resolves most of the problems that plague the other two numbering systems. This is the reason it has been almost universally adopted by history museums in the United States today.

These three systems have withstood the test of time and will fit any museum situation. There is no reason for you to reinvent the wheel and develop your own system when these are perfectly acceptable.[3]

WHICH SYSTEM SHOULD YOU USE?

It is very difficult to advise anyone on which system to use without actually seeing the museum, talking to the people involved, and looking at the rationale of the collection. I would suggest considering these factors in selecting the numbering system you should use.

The single-number system will best fit a small volunteer-run museum with a small collection and no real potential for growth. The system is simple to understand and administer. You can grasp the whole system with a quick glance in the records. If the collection should grow, or circumstances should change, the numbering system can always be changed to one of the other two systems.

- The two-number system will best fit a museum where the museum has a small collection or the accessions are infrequent and small in size. An example where this system would be useful is a museum of historical paintings that has 250 items in the collection and acquires only eight or ten accessions each year.
- The three-number system should be used in all other situations. This system is flexible and fits a variety of circumstances that come up every year in an active museum collection. The three-number system is standard in the history museum field and is readily understandable to museum professionals.

Contrary to what some people believe, the two-number and three-number systems will easily fit into most computer programs and can be easily sorted.

COLLECTION NUMBERS

The control number can convey a lot of information and does not always have to represent the year of acquisition. It can be used to correct an anomaly in the system, as a collection number, or it can indicate a change in collection practices.

It is very common in older museums to have separate and distinctly defined collections existing inside the museum collection. Sometimes there is a good reason to separate these collections, if only in the registration system. Perhaps the museum was once two separate and distinct institutions that have merged. Perhaps one was a schoolhouse museum and the other a mansion. They each have collections that should be kept apart, at least on paper.

One can identify these collections by several means. A collection number is usually a prefix on an existing number. It might look like this:

M32   S32
M32.1   S32.1
M32.1.1   S32.1.1

or

1.32   2.32
1.32.1   2.32.1
1.32.1.1   2.32.1.1

In these examples the "M" or "1" stands for "mansion" and the "S" or "2" stands for schoolhouse. With either of these systems, you can easily tell an item from one collection from an item from another, but you must be careful to avoid confusing one number with another. The letter version is a little shorter and more understandable and is favored for that reason.

The collection number does not have to be a prefix but can be indicated by the year or the control number. I list several examples below.

The reason for discussing a collection number at all in a book aimed at small museums is that it is very common to find complete collections of known provenance already existing in the museum collection which, for one reason or another, have to be kept distinct from the rest of the collection. A typical example is a museum that is the successor of a DAR (Daughters of the American Revolution) museum. There is a requirement that the DAR museum be kept distinct from the successor museum's collection, at least in the records.

Someone gave the museum a collection of stuffed birds in 1910 and a log house museum and its contents in 1933. The museum was given a defunct school system museum in 1956. They completely modernized their registration system in 1962. If you think I'm exaggerating, I am describing a collection I once administered (with the exception of the log house) along with thirty years of bad record keeping.

It is better to assign a control number than a collection number. In this case, the year of the accession is used as the control number. It would be an "artificial" year. All things considered, a control number is a collection number. Using the examples given above, you would assign a separate control number for each collection. If you found these numbers in your collection, then you would know quite a bit about the object.

909.26.XX (from the DAR museum founded in 1909)

910.26.XX (from the bird collection given in 1910)

933.26.XX (from the log cabin museum given in 1933)

956.26.XX (from the defunct school system museum given in 1956)

961.26.XX (from the museum collection before the modern registration system, which was started in 1962 but does not contain any of the known collections listed above)

[From here on in, one would use the year of accession for the year number.]

962.26.XX (from the modern museum registration system adopted in 1962)

This arrangement will work best with the two- or three-number system, which may be one reason for adopting one of these systems. A version of this system can be used with the single-number system, using controls with the earlier collections and a single number with the new accessions.[4]

USING A NUMBER TO INDICATE SPECIAL CONDITIONS

Another use of special numbering techniques in a registration system is to indicate certain characteristics of the collection. If you have large numbers of objects that are "unknown" or "found in the collection," a special source number may be a way of indicating them. If you give all of the unknowns the accession number "1" (one) each year, then they will be readily apparent. A number such as 009.1.34 will tell you that the object is of unknown origin. In some museums, they will use a "00" (double zero) instead of "1" (one). Which number you use does not matter as long as you are consistent.

We used a system at Old Economy Village.[5] In 1965 the whole collection was of "unknown" origin. It had all been acquired in 1938, but only a partial registration of the collections had been made. There had been some unrecorded acquisitions later. We gave all unknowns the control number "1," with the exception of Harmony Society–related items, which were later given the control number "2." Examples would be:

75.1.XX (object of unknown origin in the collection)

75.2.XX (unknown object of presumed Harmony Society manufacture or use)

75.3.XX (an acquisition that was accessioned using normal practices), *seratium*

Accounting for unknowns in this fashion does not relieve you from eventually having to get good title to them.

ACCESSION LEDGERS

It was common practice for museums in the eighteenth, nineteenth, and early twentieth centuries to have accession ledgers. These ledgers are usually bound record books in which the objects are usually listed in the order of acquisition. These ledgers were a combination of register and accession record. The ledgers often contain the name of the object, a brief description, and the name of the source. There is, more often than not, a number assigned to each object. These accession ledgers, if well kept, were considered quite adequate for the time and can be the basis of a good registration system even today. There are large modern museums that are presently still using a form of accession ledger and doing quite well. I am going to recommend using a version of it in the bound accession records. You have to recognize that an electronic file in a computer is a form of digital ledger. Although some museums find the computer record to be sufficient, many still keep the actual ledger so that there is a paper backup.

In the case where no number is assigned to the object in the ledger, you should make a working copy of the ledger and number the objects sequentially beginning at the front of the book. As you find objects, you can put the number that belongs on the object. The two- and three-number systems work best in these cases. If a number has been assigned in the ledger, use that number. If there are inconsistencies, you will have to work them out. Be sure not to use the original book, as it is a primary record. Make a copy.

Registers, especially those used to track accession numbers, and ledgers are discussed in the next chapter.

HOW TO HANDLE THE CENTURIES

If the museum's collection predates the twenty-first century, as many do, there must be a way to tell one century apart from another. The most common way to handle this is to assign the whole year to the accession number:

1786.32.3   1886.32.3   1986.32.3   2086.32.3

or

786.32.3   886.32.3   986.32.3   086.32.3

With this system, you can easily tell in which century the object was accessioned. A single-number system does not require any adjustment for centuries.

DEALING WITH PAIRS AND PARTS

A certain question will come up before you get very far into registering the collection: What do you do about pairs and sets? These are such things as pairs of shoes or stockings, a cup and saucer, a pair of andirons, a chess set, and so forth. It is common practice to number small sets or suites using letters. This practice of using letters to indicate a set is applied mainly to objects that will normally always be associated with each other and where there are only two or three pieces in the set, such as gloves and shoes. If you have a set of dishes with 153 pieces, letters will not work well.

I have seen people attempt to put letters in the cases of larger sets, but it often gets confusing. The question of what to do when you have more than twenty-six pieces comes up, and then awkward solutions such as double letters occur. In this case, it can get very confusing when you have 2016.1.1a and 2016.1.1aa.

In larger sets of objects, such as dining room chairs or silverware, you should number each object individually. Although strongly associated with each other, the pieces may not always be kept together. Numbering these pieces with the same number and a letter may cause problems when you only put a few of the items on exhibit or you need to store the items separately because of space issues. In these instances, it can be confusing to have all of the chairs have the same number and then label each one separately as "A," "B," and so on. By giving each a separate number, you make tracking the items for inventory, exhibition, and storage easier.

A common practice in collections is to do something like this:

1988.12.2A   Teapot
1988.12.2B   Teapot lid

Notice that I use capital letters. When the accession number is written on the object, capital letters are less easily confused with numbers than lowercase letters. Lowercase letters such as "b," "a," or "d" can often look like the number six (6), and the letter "f" can sometimes be confused with a "5" or "2."

Sometimes people choose to use numbers to define the pieces and parts instead of letters. The advantage of this is that you can account for more than twenty-six items in a set. The disadvantage is that you may be tempted to use it for sets that should be split up, like a set of dishes. An example of this system is:

1988.12.1.1   Teapot
1988.12.1.2   Teapot lid

This can sometimes be confusing for the user, and I do not recommend the latter system.

Ultimately the use of letters or numbers to define the pieces and parts is a decision you will have to make for your collection. Take some time and think about how you are going to define what gets a part number. Once you make that decision, write it down in your collections manual. This way everyone in your institution handles these items the same way.[6]

LOAN NUMBERS

While we are discussing numbering systems I will briefly go over the loan number. We will be covering loans and the need for the loan number in more depth in chapter 7. However, it is important to consider the loan number and what it will look like while you are setting up your numbering systems.

It is important that whatever numbering system you set up for your loans looks different from your accession number. That way the two systems do not get confused. Once common practice is to reverse the accession number to get the loan number. For example:

Accession number   Loan number
1986.23.2   2.23.1986

With this system, however, you will run the risk of getting the two numbers confused at some point. The best method is to place the letter "L" (for "loan") in front of the loan number and change the order in which you list the numbers:

Accession number   Loan number
1986.23.2   L2.23.1986

Another example of reordering the numbers to consider is:

Accession number   Loan number
1986.23.2   L23-1986.2

In both of these examples, you can tell that the piece is the second object in the twenty-third loan in the year 1986. There will be less confusion with the accession number because of the letter "L." I personally prefer the latter example because it looks the least like the accession number and leaves fewer chances for confusion. An example of a loan ledger is shown in the appendix.

THE DIFFERENCE BETWEEN A TEMPORARY CUSTODY, ACCESSION, REGISTRATION, CATALOG, AND CLASSIFICATION NUMBER

Some people place a great deal of significance on the number and almost treat it as a mystical thing. The only purpose of the number is to give you a handy method of identifying an object. Without the number, you would have to store the information with each object which is an inefficient way of finding both the item and its information.

Let's look at a few of the numbers that are used to track items in the collections.

Temporary custody—This is a number assigned to a collection of items when it first enters the museum under a receipt of temporary custody. These receipts may be issued for potential donations, loans, and so on. This is a temporary tracking number used until the piece(s) are registered in the accession register or loan register. It gives you a means of linking the item(s) to the donor. This is not used in all museums.

Accession number—The number assigned to an item entering the permanent collection as it is being accessioned. This becomes the tracking number for the item throughout the records in the museum.

Registration number—This is a number assigned to an item entering the museum. This term is used interchangeably with the Temporary Custody number or Accession number. See the definitions above.

Classification number—Objects are usually classified in history museums based on how the object is used. The classification number often goes to a grouping of like objects and often does not lead to an individual object but a set of like items.

Catalog/catalogue number—The purpose of the catalog number is to classify and identify the object for you by the number alone. This often has a signifier such as a letter that leads you to the classification, such as "T" for textiles, and then a number. The numbers are often assigned like a single-number accession system.

Accession vs. Catalog number

One commonly asked question in museums is: Do I need both a catalog and an accession number? The simple answer is no. With the introduction of computers into the museum the accession number can help track the item fairly easily.

Catalog numbers are useful if your system is based on classification. An example is a card catalog. With a card catalog system, it is important to be able to find the type of object and then you find the object within that classification. Please note that even with this type of system, the accession number should be listed on your card so that it can be cross referenced with the accession records.

Keep in mind, the more numbers you add for an object the more that you have to keep up with. The best idea is to follow the KISS method (keep it simple, stupid).

Many people look at library catalogs and wonder why the same type of system will not work in a museum. A library classifies a book by its subject, and arranges the book alphabetically by author inside that classification. The difference between our system and the one libraries use is that the library number, in most cases, indicates where the book is shelved, something that will not work in a museum.[7]

NUMBERS AND COMPUTERS

A computer can process almost any kind of accession number and, better yet, handle several different numbering systems at once.

However, the numbering system used in a museum and the computer often come into conflict. The problem is not in the entry; it is in the computer. You can create a field that will take anything you create on a keyboard. The problem is getting this to sort into some sort of logical sequence. Most computer programs will logically sort accession numbers, but sometimes you can still find sorting issues. There is a solution for those that won't.

If you have a field with six figures (xxxxxx) and put the number in the first field (1xxxxx), the computer treats this as the number 100,000 instead of 1. These programs may need you to enter leading zeroes to sort properly. This would mean entering the number "1" as "000001."

Letters can also cause sorting issues, as lowercase and uppercase letters may be treated differently by the program. This is why you need to make sure you have a system for letters that everyone can agree on and write it down in your collections manual.

In some cases, the periods in accession numbers may also cause problems in sorting, as they are treated as symbols or letters instead of numbers.

The most important thing is to make sure that the field you are using for your accession number will sort the information you are entering properly. More and more computer programs are designed to get around this problem. However, it is one of the questions you should ask when purchasing your collections management system.

NUMBERING DIGITAL IMAGES

Digital images have a problem in that the camera may arbitrarily assign a file number to each image. The best practice is to change the file number to the accession number. That way the image number can lead you back to the correct file.

Another way of making sure that the image is properly related to the file is to include the accession number in the photograph. You can do this by writing the number on a card or use number magnets to photograph the number with the item. Another option is to see if you can watermark the accession number onto the digital file.

If you are dealing with multiple images of the same object, it is best to have a numbering protocol for those images. The numbering should still include the accession number but may include other information such as the type of file. You can do this by adding a "C" for condition photos, an "M" for a master file, and so on. You should include this information in your collections manual.

The number can also be recorded in the metadata for the image along with other information such as when the photograph was taken and who it was taken by.

OTHER TYPES OF NUMBERING SYSTEMS

The numbering systems I have described work well with a history museum collection. There are other numbering systems that have been developed for books, archives, archaeological specimens, and so forth. Science museums have various methods that fit their varied collections. When assigning numbers to these specialized collections, it is best to use a system common to the discipline. However, if you have a small collection of such objects, it may not pay to set up a separate numbering system for just a few objects. As an example, at Old Economy we accessioned books that were part of the collection using a standard museum system and using the Library of Congress system on the reference books.

For some museums, such as small historical societies, you may have library, archival, and object collections. The accession number can be your registration number tying these collections together even if your institution uses different catalog numbering systems for these different types of items. At the Kentucky Historical Society, they use a similar system in which the accession number is assigned when the items enter the institution, but the library and archives use numbering systems that they have developed for those types of collections over the years.

SHOULD I RENUMBER MY COLLECTION?

Now that we have discussed setting up a system if there is not one already, let's turn to another common question: "Should I renumber my entire collection?" This is always a difficult question to answer without seeing the system that is in place in a museum. There are certain circumstances where renumbering a collection makes sense but most of the time it is better to work with the system you have.

Here are a few things to consider before renumbering your collection:

- Have you found all of the records/people that can explain the old system to you?
- Is there a way of "fixing" the old system?
- How many items are in the collection?
- What are your resources for doing this project?
- Save the old numbers and information.

Have You Found All of the Records/People?

Renumbering your collection should never be undertaken without a complete understanding of the existing system. If you have searched out all of the records and spoken to all of the prior caretakers whom you can find, then you have done your due diligence. If you have not, go back to square one.

These records and people may be able to explain why certain things were done with the registration system. They may be able to help you understand what you have and help you find a way to "fix" the system without renumbering the entire thing.

You also never know what some of the people may have at their house. If they had some concern about a leaking roof or similar problem, they may have taken records home for safekeeping. Although we would like to believe this never happens, there are circumstances when the volunteer or staff member may have thought it was safer to store some records offsite. They were doing the best that they could under those circumstances, so don't judge them—just ask if they can tell you anything about the system or know of any other records that may exist.

Can You "Fix" It?

Is there something you can do to fix the system? Before you try and "fix" it, do everything you can to learn about the system you have. Fixing the system can sometimes cause other problems to pop up.

For example, at the Kentucky Historical Society we had a catalog card system that hadn't been used in years. In my attempt to "fix" a problem with missing catalog cards I decided to have my volunteers refile the cards back into the accession files. The project had barely started when I learned that those catalog cards were the best clue I had to finding "found in collections" items during our wall-to-wall inventory. I stopped the filing project and recorded what happened so future registrars will know what happened with that project.

How Many Items Are in Your Collection?

Many people take on the project of renumbering their collection without considering the fact that they will need to physically renumber every item. This will take time and resources that you may or may not have. Can the system you have work, or are you willing to renumber everything both in the files and on the objects? This answer may be very different if you are dealing with 100 objects or 10,000.

What Are Your Resources for Doing This Project?

Before you start, you should look not only at the size of your collection but also at the resources you have for getting the project done. How much time will it take to renumber the collection? How many people do you have to work on it? Can you get volunteers or other staff to help? If so, what training will you have to offer them? What is your budget?

These are just a few of the questions you should ask yourself before starting a renumbering project. These questions go to your ability to actually get the project done. If you cannot complete the project, it may be better to see if you can "fix" the old system.

Save Old Numbers and Information

If you renumber the collection, you will also need to record those old numbers for later cross-referencing. Many databases have a field for "old numbers"; if yours does, use it! If it does not, find a field that you can use to record this number. This may be important later if you find a record or an object with the old number on it.

Be sure you go back to the old files and write the new number on the records. This way the paperwork is cross-referenced and you will be able to find it in the future.

Record what you know about the old system where it can be easily found. This may be an appendix to a registration or collections management manual. By recording what you know, why you made the change, and what the new system is, you have saved those following you from doing the same extensive search for information.

CONCLUSION

When beginning or updating a registration system it is important to spend a little time developing the numbering system that suits your situation. The system can make it a lot easier on you later. There is nothing particularly complicated about numbering systems. If they are well thought out, they tend to maintain themselves, once they are in place. They can affect the ease of entering data and accessioning. It is wise to set up a system that meets your needs rather than adopt someone else's system. There is nothing to stop you from adopting a new numbering system as your needs change, although I would caution you against renumbering the whole collection.

NOTES

1. Rebecca Buck, "Numbering," in Buck and Gilmore, *MRM5*, 206–8.

2. An example of a registration system using catalog numbers can be seen in the system used by the National Park Service. The park service uses a single-number system for its accession number and another single number system for its catalog number, which must cause endless confusion when these two sets of numbers inevitably equal each other. They have taken some steps to solve this problem. Buck and Gilmore, *MRM5*, use the word "catalog" or "catalogue" only for cards or sheets.

3. A number of my friends feel the three-number system was developed to account for the source of the object, but I feel it was developed to resolve the problems of the other two systems. The problem with the single-number and two-number systems would not be great if you were using only a ledger, but the three-number system works better with cards and computers.

4. A good example of the need for a collection number can be seen in the Pennsylvania Historical and Museum Commission. The PHMC has about sixty separate historic sites and museums, some of which have collections that are made distinct by law. The PHMC assigns a two-letter code to each site or museum (Old Economy is "OE," and the number would be OE67.23.9). A master number was kept by the registrar, but this did not appear on the object. A well-designed computer program can obviate the need for collection numbers.

5. Old Economy Village is a historic-site museum in Ambridge, Pennsylvania, founded by the Harmony Society in 1824 and administered by the Pennsylvania Historical and Museum Commission.

6. In 1992 at the MAAM conference, Sue Hanna, then collections manager at the Pennsylvania Historical and Museum Commission, argued during a presentation on cataloging that if all of the parts on a piece have letters, you can instantly tell that there is a piece missing should the parts get separated.

7. Buck and Gilmore, *MRM5*, have a brief discussion of numbers, 206–8.

4

Accessioning

Accessioning: A formal process used to accept legally and to record a specimen or artifact as a collection item (Malaro, 1998); involves the creation of an immediate, brief and permanent record utilizing a control number or unique identifier for objects added to the collection from the same source at the same time, for which the museum accepts custody, right, or title.[1]

The second stage of registration is the accessioning process. To accession an object means to take it into the museum's collection. This is a serious step.

Before the object is accessioned, it is a piece of property with which the owners can do anything they wish. They can give it to their Uncle Charley, destroy it, paint it green, or put it out in the barn. A property (such as a vacuum cleaner) is a depreciable item whose life is measured by the accounting practices of the museum. Property will eventually be disposed of with very few regrets or complications.

An accession is a different matter. Once an object is accessioned into a museum collection it takes on a whole new life. It becomes something that is protected by law and custom. An accessioned object is meant to be given highly specialized care and kept forever. Disposing of it, called deaccessioning, is a complicated process that takes a considerable amount of time and effort and may result in an adverse public controversy.[2]

It is wise therefore to have a well-thought-out accession policy that is strictly applied. The reason for having a sound accession policy is that it means you have fewer chances of accessioning an object that you will later have to deaccession. You must have a sound deaccession policy as well.

The accessioning process consists of making a place for the object in the museum registration system and creating a permanent record of it. The accessioning process consists of the following steps:

1. Acquiring right and title to the object. (See chapter 2 for information on this process.)
2. Assigning an accession number. (See chapter 3 for information on numbering systems.)
3. Making a record of the object.
4. Marking the object.

These actions are usually done all at once, but each is a separate process. It is important that the object be accessioned almost immediately after the museum takes possession of it, or some of the information that comes with it will be lost.

CREATING A RECORD FOR THE OBJECT

Each record must have a primary record of its existence. This is usually called the "accession record." It is created from a worksheet or a screen in the electronic record. Each of these individual records should be distinct from all the others. It should follow a format so that the same type of information is recorded for each object and so that the information is adequate. You can have many problems if you assign more than one donation to a record, have gaps in the sequence, misnumber the object, or do not record enough information. I am not going to go into all of the problems, but almost all difficulties with records start with poor accession practices.

THE REGISTER

The register is a permanent and unalterable way of recording the number sequence. The register can be created in a number of ways. (See table 4.1 for an example.)

Manual Systems

With a manual system, it is recommended that the information should be in a bound record book that keeps the whole list of accessions for the museum in the proper sequence. You can have a separate register, or use a ledger, which I will discuss below, in its place. With paper records, I prefer to keep a separate accession register, but if you can keep good control over the ledger, it is not necessary.

The purpose of the register is to keep your accessions in order so it need not carry much information. All that is necessary is the accession number, a brief description of the accession, the source, and the date. Entry into the register should be made at the time that the accession is recorded. If you let it go, you may find it difficult to complete the entries accurately later. The register acts as a catalog of all the accessions stored by number.[3]

Computer Systems

A computer system can generate its own register. Some institutions generate the register in the computer and later print it to have a paper copy as a backup. Some institutions use a log, or a paper notebook or notepad with a list of numbers on it, to verify that each accession did get entered into the computer with no gaps or duplicates. The log is not essential, but it can be a helpful tool.

Table 4.1. Computer-Generated Register Page. (The register keeps track of the accession number. The computer-generated register is faster to produce than the manual register and handy in making inventories.)

Accession #	Object Name	Material	Date	Location		Source
2003.2.1	Kit, Gun Cleaning	bronze; plastic; cotton; nylon;	ca. 1982	1053	1R	Smither, Mr. and Mrs. Thomas
2003.2.2	Net, Mosquito	nylon,	ca. 1982	1505	2	Smither, Mr. and Mrs. Thomas
2003.2.3	Uniform		ca. 1982	1505	1	Smither, Mr. and Mrs. Thomas
2003.2.4	Underpants, Long	polypropylene	ca. 1982	1505	2	Smither, Mr. and Mrs. Thomas
2003.2.5	Net, Helmet	nylon	ca.1982	2504	5	Smither, Mr. and Mrs. Thomas
2003.2.6	Shovel	plastic, metal	ca. 1985	1039	4	Smither, Mr. and Mrs. Thomas
2003.2.7	Glove	cotton/leather/wool	ca. 1982	2517	5	Smither, Mr. and Mrs. Thomas
2003.2.8	Galosh	rubber/metal/nylon	ca. 1982	2025	2R	Smither, Mr. and Mrs. Thomas
2003.2.9	Beret	wool/leather/nylon	ca. 1982	2512	8R	Smither, Mr. and Mrs. Thomas
2003.2.10	Uniform	cotton; nylon;	ca. 1982	1505	2	Smither, Mr. and Mrs. Thomas
2003.2.11	Uniform	cotton; nylon; carbon fiber;	ca. 1982	1505	2	Smither, Mr. and Mrs. Thomas
2003.2.12	Liner, Helmet	cotton; nylon	ca. 1982	2504	4	Smither, Mr. and Mrs. Thomas
2003.2.13	Undershirt	cotton	ca. 1982	1505	1	Smither, Mr. and Mrs. Thomas
2003.2.14	Mirror, Signaling	plastic; glass;	ca. 1982	1068	4L	Smither, Mr. and Mrs. Thomas
2003.2.15	Sock	polyester/cotton	ca. 1982	2517	5	Smither, Mr. and Mrs. Thomas
2003.2.16	Boot	canvas; rubber; nylon; metal	ca. 1984	2027	1L	Smither, Mr. and Mrs. Thomas
2003.2.17	Boot	leather; nylon; rubber; metal	ca. 1982	2027	3R	Smither, Mr. and Mrs. Thomas
2003.2.18	Belt, Accessory	nylon, plastic, metal	ca. 1982	1068	4L	Smither, Mr. and Mrs. Thomas
2003.2.19	Compass	plastic; nylon; water	ca. 1982	1068	4L	Smither, Mr. and Mrs. Thomas
2003.2.20	Compass	aluminum; plastic; cotton; hydrogen	ca.1982	1068	4L	Smither, Mr. and Mrs. Thomas

Courtesy of the Kentucky Historical Society

THE WORKSHEET

There has to be a way to capture the information on the object and put it in your records. At one time this would have been a worksheet. This worksheet contained all of the fields you needed to capture for a complete record. The paper worksheet has mostly been replaced by a screen in the computer program. However, some museums still use the paper worksheet, which is filled in by an expert and used by a less experienced person to complete the data entry into the database. This is a viable alternative if you do not have a computer in every area or a laptop that you can take to the piece. (See figure 4.1.)

THE HERO COUNTY HISTORICAL SOCIETY
WORKSHEET

Accession Number:

Old Number:

Title of Object:

Classification:

How acquired:

Source:

Value: Image no.

Description:

Maker:

Material:

Size:

Place of origin:

Association:

Condition:

Comments:

Current location: Location date:

2008.21

FIGURE 4.1.
The worksheet captures all the information you need to accession the object. You should arrange the fields in the order you enter them in the ledger or database. If you do not track certain data, such as value, you need not include it. This same sheet can act as a permanent accession record.

THE LEDGER

The ledger is all the accession information gathered into one place. The old museum ledgers were bound books. If complete and accurate, these bound books were excellent devices that kept all of the museum registration information in one place. It might be almost impossible to easily extract information from them, but they did store records better than any other system, even a computer. Some museums use them to this day, in many cases generating them by a computer. I am strongly recommending that you have some type of accession ledger whether paper or digital. Your worksheet is a good model for a ledger page. (In some museums this may be called a catalog; see "Capturing the Information" below.)

Manual Systems

There are several methods of creating a ledger manually. The easiest way is to type up your accession sheets and bind these periodically, say once a year. This method has the advantage that the technology is simple and cheap.

An older technology is to write the ledger information in a bound book. This may sound dreadfully old fashioned, but for very small museums this method may be a viable alternative. Use India or indelible ink on good paper. An example of a typed ledger page can be found in the appendix.

It is not a good idea to place all of the accession sheets in a file and call that a ledger. Loose files are easily disturbed, records lost, and the whole file misplaced. One of the reasons I recommend a bound book is the ability of these books to survive almost any disaster.

It is possible to type your accession sheets in a word-processing program and create the ledger from that file. This is not a good practice. If you are going to type the accession sheets up and place them in your database program, then you can easily access the information later. You can do many more things with the information than you could do with it if you typed it into a word-processing program.

Computer-Generated Ledger

Generating a ledger entry from a computer database is a relatively easy process with almost any program. (See figure 4.2.)

Whether it is practical to print all your data out is another matter. If you have ten thousand objects, the ledger may very well be ten thousand pages long. Bound at 250 pages per book, this is forty volumes. As the ultimate backup, this may be a very useful project, but it is a big project that may not be too practical. Since computer files are constantly updated this printed ledger can be considered a snapshot of the collection at one point in time. But what happens if you have fifteen thousand objects (sixty volumes), or twenty-five thousand objects (one hundred volumes)? There are computer service companies that will be able to print this out for you. However, an electronic backup may be a more practical solution to printing the pages.

Remember this: Data stored in an electronic form deteriorates over time, and computer programs change at a faster and faster rate. The life of a computer program is typically about five years, and companies often do not "support" them after the new version of the software comes out. Without the program, you may not be able to read the data. If printed on good paper, the written record lasts almost forever. It may pay to print out your whole file once in a lifetime, even if you have a huge collection.

CAPTURING THE INFORMATION

Some museums divide the accession information on the object into two separate categories of accession and catalog information. Whether this difference has any meaning to a small museum is a moot point, but all this information should be written down at the time the object is accessioned. This information is gathered on a worksheet or entered directly into the database.

Objects Summary

01/17/2017   *Matches 76*

Catalog / Objectid / Objname	Description	Condition	Status	Home Location
O 2003.2.1 Kit, Gun Cleaning	This is an Army rifle cleaning kit. Part a) is an olive drab case for the maintenance equipment for a M16A1 rifle. The case has two pockets with velcro closures which is enclosed by a three snap button flap and belt clip. Parts b and c) are cleaning brushes that have olive drab plastic handles with a cast grip. Part d) is the handle of the cleaning rod with one tapped end. Part e) is a rolled metal rod with a flattened end with nylon bristles. Part f) is a chamber brush with a twisted steel and bronze bristles with cardboard protector. One end of the brush is black plastic with a ratchet end and four tapped holes. Parts g-k) are steel cleaning rod extensions tapped on one end and threaded on the other. Part l) is a bore brush with bronze bristles for .223 caliber. Parts m and n) are steel patch cleaners threaded on one end and slotted on the other. Part o) is a ziploc package of cleaning swabs.	Good	Record Updated	HC MS 1053 1R
O 2003.2.2 Net, Mosquito	This is an Army mosquito net. It is an olive green nylon mosquito net tent cover with reinforced corners and nylon tie downs.	Good	Record Updated	HC MSM 1505 2 40-119
O 2003.2.3 Uniform	This is an Army chemical uniform. It is a size medium. Part a) is a woodland camouflage pattern jacket with a rounded collar. It has two angled front patch breast pockets with velcro closures. There is elastic at the sleeve cuffs. There is a zip front closure covered with three snap buttons and a drawstring around the waist. There are three snaps in the back just below the belt loops. There are adjustable straps on both sides of the waistband. Part b) is a pair of woodland camouflage pattern pants. It has a zip closure with one snap. There are two front patch pockets with velcro closures at the thigh level. There are velcro and zipper side closures on each leg running up to the pocket. There are drawstring closures at the pants cuffs. There are three snap buttons below the belt loops and there are straps for an adjustable waistband on each side.	Excellent	Record Updated	HC MSM 1505 1 40-117
O 2003.2.4 Underpants, Long	This is a pair of Army thermal underwear bottoms. They are a full length brown thermal underwear size large. There is an elastic waistband excessive wear around crotch area; three holes of varying size high on right leg.	Fair	Record Updated	HC MSM 1505 2

FIGURE 4.2.
The ledger information is mostly gathered at the time the object is accessioned. The ledger in a manual system is the worksheet information gathered in a book form. In this example, the information is in a database and accessed on a screen. It may or may not be printed out.
Courtesy of the Kentucky Historical Society

Museums have discussed designing a system for history museums that would define common fields or terminology for history museums. Of course, the Chenhall nomenclature system exists and has been revised multiple times for object names but what about the rest of the fields in the database? In the late 1980s, the Common Agenda Data Bases Task Force looked into the issue. This was the first real attempt to develop a system that had a standard definition of data fields common to all history museums.[4] Not much further work has been done on the concept since, but it was a worthwhile project and very usable.

Accession Information

The accession information needed is relatively simple. One needs only:

1. Name of the object
2. Source (name of donor or vendor)

3. Any restrictions or limit on the accession
4. Value (if the museum collects that information)
5. Size
6. Description
7. Date of acquisition
8. Location
9. An image if you are taking pictures

Catalog Information

One acquires catalog information through discussions with the source of the accession, by examination of the object itself, and through research. The Common Agenda Data Base Task Force separated catalog information into descriptive data and historical data. Whatever you call it, the best time to capture it is at the time of the accession. (See chapter 6 on cataloging.)

The reason for making a point about the difference between catalog and accession data is that in some museums two different departments involving two different people might be responsible for collecting this data. The small museum seldom has to worry about this sort of thing.

As part of the capture of all the information associated with the object the museum should develop a record form that has a field for each discrete piece of information. A field is one particular piece of information such as the accession number, name of the object, or the date of manufacture. I suggest some fields in the chapter on computers. The task force divided the data into major groups of fields.

Management Data

This is, according to the task force's definition, "data normally recorded or created when an object comes into a collection, and data recorded as a means of relating objects and records to one another." This information is what museums call "accession" data.

Descriptive Data

The definition of this information is "data that can be gathered about an object by observing it or by applying fairly simple research techniques, such as discovering an object's name or title." I like to think that this is information the object itself tells you. This information is what some museums would call "catalog" data.

Historical Data

Historical data is described as "data that provides a historical context for objects, relating them to people, organizations, places, events, and concepts." This is the data that is the hardest to acquire but is the most important. I discuss historical data in chapter 5, "Documentation."

DESCRIPTIONS

There is quite a difference between descriptive information written for a manual record and one for a computer. For paper records, compactness and succinctness is a plus. The information is concentrated rather than expanded. A computer may not be able to read a number of abbreviations or handle cryptic notes such as "somewhat like 22.8.6." The computer may well look on such things as a pair of andirons as one object, but with a paper record you can easily distinguish that there are two objects.

The information below is mainly for manual records although useful for both media. For a computer record, some of the information, such as size, classification, name, provenance, and so on, would go in separate fields. I discuss this in chapter 8, "A World of Computers."

This basic part of the record of a properly registered object is the description. Descriptions should be simple and short but complete enough to be used in court. If you follow the journalistic who, what, where, when, and why, you will have a fairly complete description. If you always describe objects using the same criteria in the same order, you will not miss much and all your descriptions will be complete. If you set up a data table, it makes things easier. A worksheet will do this for you. The computer essentially sets up a data table on screen with all its separate fields such as:

Nomenclature: Table, Dining

Classification: Category 2: Furniture

Provenance: New England, perhaps made in Zeus. In Jones family since before 1858. William Jones IV, donor.

Association: Jones family; donor says William Jones (I) wrote the town charter on table, ca. 1858.

Date: 1810–1830

Description: Four inside-tapered legs; rectangular top; outside batten, flush drawer; brass mushroom pulls; stained and varnished.

Material: walnut; poplar; brass

Condition: excellent

Other information: Exhibited in NY Furniture Society exhibit "The New York Cabinetmaker," 1924; catalogue in acc. File. Hepplewhite style.

Size: 64½"w × 38¼"d × 29½"h.

If written in manual system as a description, it might look like the sample below. In a computer, the information would be in several different fields (as shown above).

005.26.1 Table, dining: New England, early nineteenth century (1810–1830); perhaps local in manufacture; Jones family association; donor says grandfather (William Jones, 1822–1908) wrote Zeus town charter on this table in ca. 1858; Hepplewhite style; four inside-tapered legs; rectangular top; outside batten; flush drawer with brass mushroom pulls; walnut; stained and varnished; excellent condition; exhibited in the New York Furniture Society exhibit, "The New York Cabinetmaker, 1924"; see catalogue in accession file; see also probate of Adam Jones will in courthouse; 64½"w × 38¼"d × 29½"h.

Notice that I qualified several statements in this accession. I used the statement "donor says . . ." An oral tradition about 150 years old is suspect, but it has been in his family. The donor did not know the exact dates of his grandfather's life, but what information was available is given so that details can be checked later. When I did not know the exact date, I used "ca." for "circa," which means "about."

It is a good idea to do the research on each object as it comes in, before the registration process is completed. The dates his grandfather lived and worked, the courthouse records on its construction, and construction techniques available at the time all should have been researched. The typical small museum may not have the time to do all this when the accession is made, but the bones of the research will be there, if captured in the first place, and will be available when needed later.

Usually, one develops a sort of laconic style, leaving out all unnecessary wording. If subject-less or verb-less statements separated by semicolons are used, the descriptions may be shorter. These in-house descriptions do not have to have any literary merit; they just have to be complete enough to identify that particular object. The descriptions should evoke an accurate picture in the reader's mind, especially if he is unfamiliar with the object. Short, succinct descriptions are best. The reader of the records has to bring some knowledge with him. The exception to this rule can occur when/if you publish your catalog online. In that case, it may be easier for the public if you use complete sentences, as that is what they are used to seeing.

Because of the use of a computer, many museums have reduced the description to a few brief comments or done away with it altogether. This is not a good practice. The first consideration is that the description offers you a way to distinguish new classes of objects. You may be able to extract such information as whether a certain class of table has flush drawers (versus lipped drawers), which may be significant when compared to other data. The computer offers you a method of making these comparisons quickly, although this can be done with much more difficulty in manual records.

The second consideration is that if the object is stolen, you have to have a description good enough to distinguish that object from all others of its type. You would be surprised how difficult it is to describe to the police how your unique handmade apple peeler is different from all the other unique handmade apple peelers.

The final reason for a description is that it helps you identify the object. For one reason or another, you may have to find objects by their descriptions rather than number or location. Using the search engines of a computer program, you can find all the objects with certain characteristics, such as outside battens.

If you adopt the policy that the condition of the object will be described as *pristine, excellent, good, fair,* or *poor* (corresponding to the marks of A, B, C, D, or E), you save some space. A good practice in manual records is to assume that all objects are in good ("C") condition unless indicated otherwise, and again you save time. On computer records it would be better to fill in the blank, as the computer will have difficulty differentiating whether a blank means "C" or nothing. Please note that this system is extremely subjective, as one person's good may be another person's excellent or fair, and a complete condition report should be done at a later date to determine the condition of the item.[5]

Measure accurately. On large objects, measure to the sixteenth of an inch, and on small ones measure to the thirty-second. Some registrars have the practice of measuring to the next largest unit of measurement. That is, if you measure $3^3/_{16}$ inches, you then record $3^1/_4$ inches. That method has a lot to recommend it. Many museums use a metric system and measure to the millimeter. Some museums put both means of measurement in their records, but that may be too much for the small museum. Adopt a policy of which system you will use so that one person does not use the inch/foot and the other the metric system. It is easy to configure most data management programs to convert one measurement to the other so that by entering an inch/foot measurement (for instance) you will automatically get the metric measurement.

It is best to take the overall outside measurements in a particular order. If you measure the width first, then the depth, and then the height, it will help to ensure consistency and simplify your work when you prepare exhibits.

The museum often receives a number of objects that are more or less identical, such as a set of dinner plates. When you are using manual records, it is best to take one object that is typical of all of them and describe it in detail. Then, for the rest, use the abbreviation *ibid.*, which stands for *ibidem* and means "in the same place."

Ibidem is a Latin word used in scholarly footnotes to refer to the citation before. Its use in the accession records refers only to the description immediately preceding it. If you have a dining room set with twelve matching side chairs, you pick the most typical chair and describe it, and then, for the others, you need only mention minor variations following the word *ibid.* (Actually, *idem,* abbreviated as *id.,* meaning "the same," would be more correct, but I am following the common practice.)

Even if the objects are not enough alike to use the term *ibid.,* it helps to line up similar objects. The similar or unique characteristics will show up immediately. If you are accessioning a group of clothing items, place all the dresses in one pile, all the coats in another, and so on, instead of just grabbing items at random as they come out of the trunk. (Although if the trunk is still in the same order the way it was originally packed, that would be of interest.) You will be amazed at the way this simple method helps descriptions.

If you use a computer program for cataloging, the use of *ibid.* will not work. Computer searches will not know to compare this record with the first in the series, at least in most programs. Even in the unlikely circumstances that the computer can make such a search, it would be slower and more prone to errors than if you just give every object its own description. However, the computer gives you the means to duplicate the information in the record or copy it into the other records where it is needed.

Describe the usual characteristics and the unusual ones that mark the object. You would be surprised how often descriptions miss the obvious, such as the number of legs on a table. Some objects, such as stamps or coins, are described in catalogs. Referring to the catalog number can simplify descriptions. Some classes of objects (such as carpenters' planes) have a standard scholarly work written about them. Making a reference to the description in that work can save time. However, make sure that future staff members will have access to that description before you do this. If this is a book in your personal collection and the next collections manager cannot find a copy of the book, this means of description is useless.

Do not make up words for technical descriptions. If you do not know what a ferrule is, call it a band of metal. Most technical terms come from only four sources: the parts of the human body, nature, mathematics, and architecture. If you learn the terminology for those four sources, you will be explicit even if you do not know the exact term. Clothing and decorative arts have a language all their own that must be learned eventually if you want accurate descriptions. Consistency and accuracy are more important than a technical vocabulary.

The worksheet that I have mentioned before will ensure that you record all the data you need in the order that you want it. A worksheet is useful when you are dealing with less knowledgeable people or people in training status. Even experienced curators will find worksheets useful. There is an example of a worksheet in the appendix. You will probably need a worksheet even if your information is stored in a computer. The worksheet does not have to be paper. It can be a screen on your computer.

MARKING OBJECTS

Almost all the work you have done so far on registering an object will go to waste if you do not put the proper accession number on the object. The number ties the object to the records. Marking the object should be part of a definite chain of actions that you perform in the registration process. The process of accessioning the object should not be considered complete until the number is on the object.[6]

Marking the object is quite a complex process. You will end up with a different technique of marking for each type of object. The marking should not be visible when the object is displayed but should be easily found otherwise. The method of marking should not damage the object. The object should not be marked on finished surfaces. Finally, the number should be firmly attached to the object, so that it will last, but be easily removable if necessary.

Where Do I Number the Item?

Places such as inside the drawer on furniture, the bottom of plates, and the waistband of garments are all logical places to place a number on an object. On tools and implements there may be a problem in finding a hidden place for the number, as the tool may be viewed from any angle. Find as unobtrusive a place as possible. On large pieces, place the number where you will not have to move the piece to find it.

It is a good idea to standardize the places that your institution numbers certain types of objects. Some types of objects will loan themselves well to a standard spot for a label (quilts, dresses, vases) while others will not (jewelry, tools, sculpture). If you can create a general guideline for a specific type of object, you can make this a listing of the guidelines in your collections management procedures. These guidelines will make it easier for every new staff member, intern, or volunteer to find the numbers on an object. The guidelines can also provide them instructions as to where they should number an object. There are always exceptions to these guidelines, but standardizing the numbering spots on similar items makes the number easy to find.

How Do I Number the Item?

How you mark each object will vary from object to object. One commonly known method that works for many objects is the "sandwich method." This process includes having a base coat that is placed on the object (usually this will be Soluvar, Acryloid B-72, or Acryloid B-67), the number (written in ink, acrylic, or even typed on acid-free paper or Mylar), and then a top layer to protect the number.

This process works for many objects with some minor variations. For instance, for a dark object, it may be difficult to read a number written in black ink. Some museums get around this by putting the base layer on the object and then either writing in white ink or using another layer of white acrylic paint on top of the base layer so that the black ink can then be seen. Some museums prefer to print the number for glass items on clear Mylar plastic. The Mylar can then be placed between the base coat and top layer on glass items so that the number is not as obtrusive while on display.

The important thing with the sandwich method is to read all instructions and warnings carefully before applying the solution. Some of the chemicals can damage the surface of an item or have a chemical reaction with the piece. This is often seen with plastics, rubber items, and the finish on painted pieces or furniture.

Always avoid look-alike materials that are not purchased from an archival supplier. I have walked into several small museums where they have used clear nail polish and white correction fluid to number their pieces. While these materials look like the labeling solutions they are not recommended by conservators and can cause damage to the objects.

Clothing and textiles do not work with the sandwich method described above. You should never mark clothing and textiles directly on the material. The best method is to use a strip of cotton twill tape, a small piece of fabric, or a small piece of Tyvek as a label. You can write the number on this label with a laundry pen. The label can then be sewn into the garment.

For clothing, I often recommend the back of the neckline on a shirt or dress and the waistband on pants or a skirt. The reason for this is that people are already used to looking for a manufacturer's label in these places. The number will not be seen while the garment is on display but it will be easily found by someone looking for it. For textiles such as quilts, coverlets, and blankets, I usually recommend sewing the label to two of the back corners. You can sew them to the corners diagonal from each other, and then it should be easy for someone to find.

Paper items should be marked with a soft pencil (#2). Many of these items can be marked on the back corner. For books, you can write the number inside the front or back cover.

Small items like coins, medallions, medals, and jewelry are always a challenge to number. Unless you are very experienced with numbering and have an extremely steady hand, you will probably not be able to number them with the sandwich method. Often it is easier to put the number on the storage materials for these items. For example, you can place a medal in a small paper envelope or a plastic bag and number the outside of the enclosure.

A small sculpture may have surfaces that cannot be marked. Items like these may have to be stored resting on a tag with its number. If this is the case, be sure to move that tag any time the item is moved, or you will lose its number.

Glued-on paper labels, especially ones that are pressure sensitive, are a very poor choice. So are labels that come out of a label maker. The adhesives break down rapidly and may damage the object. The labels also have a perverse way of dropping off at the most inconvenient moment, and then not being removable at other times. Tapes should also be avoided.

Paper tags held on with string are very useful as a second marker but not as the permanent one. You can buy acid-free ones from a number of sources such as archival suppliers. Objects in storage will be easier to find with paper tags, and that may be a reason to use them. However, they should never be considered the sole means of marking objects, as they are removed too easily.

Whatever method you chose, the numbering process should be reversible. If you are worried about causing damage to an object, call an objects conservator for a recommendation.

DEACCESSIONING

The question in deaccessioning is not if there is going to be a problem but *when* there will be one.[7]

With deaccessioning, it is the *accessioning* policy that is important. If you are careful about what you bring in, you will have fewer objects of which to dispose. The development of a sound accession policy, the careful execution of procedures, and good records will put off the evil day and lessen any problem with deaccessioning when it occurs. Moreover, there is hardly a museum in the country that does not depend on the goodwill of its audience for survival. The goodwill is often expressed in gifts to the museum. When offered objects, the museum is under an obligation to accept only what it really needs, can really take care of, has a use for, and intends to keep.[8]

There is a "Donation Assessment" form in appendix A (see A-3) that represents a procedure for evaluating objects *before* accessioning and will help the museum make the decision to accept or reject items offered to it. It is a handy form to show collection committees. Using this procedure will help you acquire objects less likely to be deaccessioned later.

No matter how carefully written the collection policy of a museum may be, or how tightly that policy is enforced, there is no museum that does not occasionally end up with objects that do not belong in the collection.

- There may be too many of one kind of object.
- The object may not fit the collection policy.
- It may have deteriorated to the point that it has lost its integrity or is a threat to the collection.
- It may be a fake (or at least not as represented).
- The museum may not be able to take care of the object properly.

Balanced against these reasons for deaccessioning are some factors that may affect whether you can deaccession and how easy the process is:

- Provisions in your organic documents, such as your charter, constitution, or by-laws, may forbid or place restrictions on your ability to deaccession.
- Your agreement with the donor may disallow deaccessioning of that particular object, which normally could be deaccessioned.

- The donor, or his or her family, may still be alive and active in the community.
- The community may have an interest in the object(s) and create a public relations problem with the deaccession.

It is a poor policy for the museum to dispose of objects in its collection unless there is an overriding reason for doing so. I would recommend not deaccessioning an object from a living donor, or one that has a known history related to your purpose, unless it is deteriorated to the point that it endangers the collection.

It is important to follow a set of procedures in deaccessioning and to be able to justify all of the steps. The "Justification for Deaccessioning" form (see textbox 4.1 and form A-14 in appendix A) makes sure that you have considered all the factors when you deaccession an object. Each of the two collection policies in the appendix has a deaccession procedure including a "Justification of Deaccessioning" form. There should be a clearly understood policy about how the object is to be disposed of. Using the form, or the procedure it represents, will help the museum have a rational method of deaccessioning and keep the collection germane to the purpose of the museum.

TEXTBOX 4.1

JUSTIFICATION FOR DEACCESSION

You have to document deaccessions very carefully and very thoroughly. The list below can serve as the basis of a deaccession form that can help all parties involved visualize the reasons for deaccessioning an object. It is based on a form developed by Bruce Bazalon, former registrar of the Pennsylvania Historical and Museum Commission.

- Reason for deaccession:
  - Duplicates another object.
  - Not germane to the collection (does not fit the collection policy).
  - It is a fake or not as represented.
  - It is in poor condition.
  - The museum cannot take care of it.
- Is the history of the object tied in any way to the purpose of the museum?
- Are there any restrictions on this object?
- Is the object part of a collection?
- Is the donor still living?
- Does the community have an interest in this object?
- What will happen to this object if it is not deaccessioned?
- What is the method of disposal?
- A place for all approvals of curator, director, collections committee, board, and so on.
- Action taken.
- Date(s) of action.

When a museum sells a deaccessioned item, it is best to do this at public auction rather than at a private sale. This keeps things in the public eye. Private sales may give the perception of favoritism and self-dealing, serious ethical charges.

The proceeds from the sales of collections should go to benefit the collection. This can be in a conservation fund, an acquisitions fund, and so on. The funds should not be used to pay off construction debts, liens, or the like. Guidelines on the use of the funds for the direct care of the collections were developed by an American Alliance of Museums taskforce on Direct Care and released in 2016.[9]

Although the museum board should reserve the right to dispose of the collection in any way it sees fit, in actual practice the museum will be rated on how much it keeps and keeps well. I could write a whole book on donor and community concerns involved in deaccessioning. The museum has to carefully consider what impact any deaccession will have on its relationship with its donors and the community. Every deaccession represents some failure on the part of the museum. However, deaccessioning is very much like pruning a tree; it hurts, but it is necessary for growth. If the museum carefully considers each deaccession, the problems will be fewer.

Deaccessioning Undocumented Objects

Undocumented objects are popularly called "found in collection" objects. You have the object, but you do not know how you got it. Just because you do not have any records of these objects does not mean you have the absolute right to dispose of them. Indeed, you may have to keep them almost forever. Some states have laws that set up a procedure for disposing of such objects. Advice from a lawyer is necessary.[10]

There is a rule in treating undocumented objects found in the collection: if they are not accessioned and you intend to dispose of them, then you do not need to accession them. It saves a lot of steps if you do not accession unknowns just to deaccession them. Disposal is much easier. It is mandatory, however, to make a list of these objects and get board approval when you dispose of them, so there is some record. You must also be very sure that these objects belong to you and are yours to dispose of. Several states have ways of acquiring title to such found-in-collections objects.

Documenting Deaccessions

When you take something into your collection, you should at the same time think about how it might be removed without creating confusion in the records. The governing body acts. The easiest way to get such action is to have the curator, through the director, recommend to the collections committee that the object be deaccessioned. The committee then makes a report to the board concerning the object, the reasons for the deaccession, and the method of disposal. If the board approves, the action is carried out.

You should not get rid of the records for the object that has been deaccessioned just because it is gone. You are still obligated to keep the record of it. For paper records, a note indicating that the object has been deaccessioned should be made in red ink in the master record. The reason for using red ink for this transaction on the records is that it will show up clearly. The type of removal (sold, destroyed, transferred), the date it happened, and the date of the action of the governing body should all be entered into the permanent record. If you have catalog cards for the deaccessioned object, they should be placed in a dead file. There should be some method in a computer record to indicate that the object has been deaccessioned, and a method of keeping it from getting mixed with the rest of the records, but, again, the record should be kept. The status field (which tells whether it is an accession, loan, etc.) is good for this purpose.

TIERED COLLECTIONS

Museums often have objects that they wish to keep but do not wish to accession. Typical examples are objects that are used in education programs or are kept for study. In these cases museums often create a tiered system. There may be anywhere from two to a dozen tiers. The museum designates one or two tiers in which the object is accessioned and cared for under the highest museum standards. Other tiers may not be technically accessioned but may be used in education programs or kept as specimens. These often get a special numbering system or no numbering system at all and may be kept in different ledgers.

This arrangement will work, but the museum has to have a very good understanding of its mission and the role of the collection. The ability to administer such a system is important. Someone has to constantly monitor the use of objects so that everyone will understand that you can use objects marked with an "X" (for example) and may not use the ones that are not.

Be aware that if you take in an object from a donor under the impression that it is to be a "museum" object and then place it in non-collection status, you have created a sizeable ethical and perhaps legal problem. Be up front with donors about the status of any object you take into your collection, whether accessioned or not.

WHAT NOT TO DO AND WHEN NOT TO DO IT

The major mistake people make is not to accession the object as soon as it comes in. If it is not accessioned properly, information will be lost, parts may turn up missing, or the object may not be accessioned at all. I have always been amazed, at the museums where I had collection responsibilities, at how many objects sat around for years without being accessioned. The final mistake is not to put the number on the object at the same time it is accessioned.

THE FINAL WORD ON ACCESSIONING

Several variations of the basic system of accessioning have been outlined here in the hope that an understanding of them will help the person in charge set up his or her own system. The important things about the system are:

- That the flow of actions be orderly and uncomplicated from the first contact until the object is displayed or stored
- That the museum be able to account for any action at any stage of the process
- That the system be consistent
- That the system has the understanding and approval of the people directing and managing the museum and be able to be carried out over a number of years through the reigns of several curators

The records of the museum are only tools meant to help you preserve and interpret the collection. Do not create a monster that will eat up the purpose of the museum in a maze of paperwork. Simplicity is the key.

NOTES

1. Stephen L. Williams, "Critical Concepts Concerning Non-Living Collections," *Collections* 1 (2004): 37–66, particularly "Accessioning" (43–45) and "Cataloging" (45–46).

2. Malaro, *Primer*, 57–247, has an extensive look at all of the things once must consider during the acquisition and accessioning process.

3. You can also get a type of record called a "minute book," which has loose pages. The pages can be permanently fixed later but can be written upon or copied until bound.

4. James C. Blackaby, Chair Common Data Bases Task Force, *Final Report to the Field, September 1989*, Common Agenda for History Museums (Nashville: American Association for State and Local History, 1989). Other sets of database standards such as the standards of the Canadian Heritage Information Network exist, but they are not directed specifically at history museums.

5. In a Connecting to Collections Care webinar titled *Basic Condition Reporting* (September 15, 2016), Deborah Rose Van Horn made an argument for not using the terms excellent, good, fair, and poor as a condition report without further description because these terms are too subjective.

6. The marking of objects is a constantly evolving technology. Tamara Johnston and Robin Meador-Woodruff, "Numbering" in Buck and Gilmore, *MRM5*, and Helen Alten, "Materials for Labeling Collections," *The Upper Midwest Museums Collections Care Network* 1, no. 6 (Winter 1996), 1–7.

7. The quote about deaccessions being a potential problem was once commonplace in the museum field. I have not heard it lately, but it remains true.

8. Stephen E. Weil, *A Deaccession Reader* (Washington, DC: American Association of Museums, 1997), passim; Phelan, *Museum Law*, 232–36; Charles Philips, "The Ins and Outs of Deaccessioning," *History News* 38 (November 1983), 6–11; Malaro, *Primer*, 248–72; Martha Morris and Antonia Moser, "Deaccessioning," in Buck and Gilmore, *MRM5*, 100–107; Rebecca Buck, "Deaccessioning Risk Chart," in Buck and Gilmore, *MRM5*, 108.

9. American Alliance of Museums, *Direct Care of Collections: Ethics, Guidelines, and Recommendations*, April 2016.

10. Buck and Gilmore, "Found in Collection," *Collections Conundrums*, 37–47. They have a state-by-state chart of laws effecting found-in-collection objects.

5

Documentation

When you acquire an object, you acquire a great deal more than the object itself. You acquire the history of the people who made or used the object. This legacy is often more valuable to the museum than the intrinsic value of the object. The very difference between a history museum and other types of museums is often that they collect objects for their historical value rather than their intrinsic, aesthetic, or scientific values. Of course, these other values are important and a major factor in history museum collection, but not the primary value. The only way to preserve this value is to write it down. The written history is the documentation of the object and the collection.

In the United States, it is a normal practice to separate registration from documentation. The usual practice is to consider that registration applies to all of the records generated in the acquisition, accession, and catalog process and that documentation applies to research developed on the object and the collection. Be aware that some people in the museum field apply the term "documentation" to all the documents developed on an accession or the collection. They expressly include the ones I separate as "registration" documents. This usage is more true of Great Britain than the United States, although the term "documentation" as applied to registration is often used here. I am separating the two terms in this book, partly to follow the common practice of the United States, and partly to avoid confusion. For the purposes of this book, "documentation" is part of the registration process, not the process itself.[1]

You acquire information on the object in two ways. Some information comes with the object. The rest is found by research.

INFORMATION THAT COMES WITH THE OBJECT

The donor or seller of an object will often furnish you with information about the object. There will often be the owner's reminiscences or family history. If you question the donor, he or she can often give you an amazing amount of background information. It is important to capture as much of this history that you can. Ask for photographs, documents, and other things related to the object. The owner will not know that they are important.

You should be aware of all the pitfalls of oral information. Nothing ever became less important or valuable over time. Still, if it is the original owner or a descendant who provides the information, it is close to the source. Almost all oral information is lost when the object is sold to a dealer or second party. Any history coming from such second-party sources is suspect, especially if it is an unsupported attribution to an owner, artist, or maker.

However unlikely some of this information may be, if you do not collect it at the time of the accession, it will be forever lost. All of it should be carefully recorded. You can check out the information later through research.

INFORMATION DISCOVERED BY RESEARCH

The museum should have an ongoing research project concerning the history covered by the museum's purpose. If your purpose is to preserve the history of Hero County, you would continually conduct research on the history of the county. Research is never completed.

You also must conduct research on the objects in the museum. Who made or used them, when they made them, and how they were used will be constant objects of research. You must also learn something about the cultural and aesthetic motives of the people who made and used the objects, and the technical qualities of the object. Research will give you a greater understanding of the people associated with your collection and be of enormous help in collecting more objects, interpretation, and exhibits.

REGISTRATION FILES VERSUS RESEARCH FILES

Even the smallest museum may have several types of documents that ought to be preserved. It is common to have the accession file that contains all the documents on each object, a research file that contains all history related to the museum's purpose, the archives that contain documents in the museum's collection, and the museum files that are business and other records.[2] There is a good reason to keep separate files, but all of these should be preserved as museum archives.

The major difference between archives and business files is the type of care they receive and how you intend to preserve them. The archives, of whatever kind, are part of the museum's collection. Although archives are used for research, they receive the highest standard of care the museum can devise. It may be stored separately, but the museum registration system is part of the museum's archives. Sometimes research files are files that do not receive the same care that the archives do. In this case, you should make sure that documents to be preserved go into the archives or at least get a high standard of care.

Documents that come with objects are part of the museum archives. If these are stored in accession files, be sure that these files follow archival standards. If the documents are used frequently, then they should be copied, the copies placed in the research files, and the originals preserved.

Some documents are as much a part of the accession as the object itself. These might be operating manuals, original letters referring to the object, photographs that show the object in use, legal documents concerning it, and so forth. You have to make a decision on which of these are accessioned, which go into the accession file, which go to the research file, and which go to the museum archives. The decision is based on the standard of care you give each file and, perhaps, who has access to it.

THE MUSEUM LIBRARY

The museum should develop a library on its collection. A small book budget will go a long way. If you collect a book here and there, eventually you will have a good reference library. Books are expensive, but many are remaindered and can be acquired cheaply. Donors are often quite generous with books. When I started at Old Economy, I had eight books in the museum reference library. When I left sixteen years later, there were more than two thousand books in the library, and I never, in that whole time, had a book budget. If I had a book budget, I would have had four thousand books. Keep at it, and eventually your efforts will show results.

PUBLISHING RESEARCH

No research is any good unless it is published. The museum publishes in many ways. Exhibits and interpretation programs can be considered a method of publication that is especially suited to a museum. Every exhibit requires some research, and if this is published, it will add another dimension to the exhibit. As simple a thing as a fact sheet will outlast the exhibit and be a permanent remainder of your research. Even if these have to be done on the office copier, they are still a publication. The museum should publish articles and monographs on its collection. Your newsletter is a good place to publish what you have found. Another way to publish is to encourage and assist outside researchers. Their publications should be added to your library.

Remember that exhibits and interpretive programs, although valuable and necessary, are ephemeral, but publications last forever.

INTEREST GROUPS

There is an interest group on almost any subject, no matter how obscure. I once subscribed to a magazine for plumb bob collectors. These groups have publications, meetings, memberships, and such. There must be at least one, if not a dozen, of these groups whose interests are aligned with those of any museum. These groups will be conversant with current research and standards in their field. They will know all the specialists in the obscure areas of their interest. They will know all the good books on their specialty and how to get discounts.

I would suggest that you join as many of these interest groups as you need and can afford. Go to as many of their meetings as you can. Their annual meetings are information factories where you can find out almost anything you need to know. You will discover the state of current knowledge when you do this.

Most of these groups also have some sort of presence on the Internet, whether it is a website, social media, or even just an email list-serv. These online forums are often free and will allow you to learn from the group or share your information with them.

INFORMATION FROM OTHER MUSEUMS

Other museums that collect in the same area as yours can be quite helpful. They will have a research file and a library. Their professional staff will be conversant with the knowledge you need. Museums lend objects as well, and they may be able to help you with exhibits.

However, it is a common experience in a large museum for someone from the Godforsaken Historical Society to show up unannounced at the most inconvenient moment and seek highly specialized knowledge. The seeker might be put off by curt answers and hasty references to standard reference works, but you can hardly expect curators to impart all the knowledge they have gained in a lifetime in twenty minutes. Contact the museum in advance, telling the staff what you would like to know, and you will usually find them very helpful.

The Internet offers museums access to a huge pool of information about objects and collections. Many museums are now putting their collections and research online to facilitate researchers. However, the amount of data out there can offer its own challenge. It is often difficult to sort through the number of records retrieved in a search to find exactly what you are looking for.

HIGHER STANDARDS

The history museum profession is now placing a much higher value on capturing the historical data on the object than it has in the past. The very nature of a history museum, of being more interested in the object's history than in the object as a specimen, makes this imperative.

WHAT NOT TO DO AND WHEN NOT TO DO IT

The first mistake is not to get all the information at the time you acquire the object. The second mistake is not to write it down. I once ran a museum with almost eighty thousand objects related to a particular culture. Each object had a story, but that story was lost, as it was in the heads of the founders, who had died thirty years before. It is a general rule that if you do not capture the information at first, it is lost forever. Since the history museum may be more interested in the history of the object than the object itself, you have an obligation to find out all you can about the object and write this down in some easily accessible form. If you have done this on every object, you may have preserved something as valuable as the object itself.

NOTES

1. The common view in the United States is that documentation is the assemblage of all the research information on the object. Europeans view it as all the documents assembled during the whole registration process. I tend to accept the former view. See Museum Documentation Association, *Practical Museum Documentation*, 2nd ed. (Duxford, Cambridgeshire, UK: Museum Documentation Association, 1981). However, one of the first practical books aimed at American museums, Carl E. Guthe, *The Management of Small History Museums*, 2nd ed. (Nashville: AASLH, 1969), 21–50, discussed the entire registration system as documentation.

2. William A. Deiss, *Museum Archives: An Introduction* (Chicago: Society of American Archivists, 1984), discusses museum archives as separate from other archives; James Summerville, "Using, Managing and Preserving the Records of Your Historical Organization," *Technical Report 11* (Nashville: AASLH, 1986).

6

The Catalog

Cataloging/Cataloguing: Creation of a full record on information about a specimen or artifact, cross-referenced to other records and files, including the process of identifying and documenting these objects in detail.[1]

The catalog, or catalogue,[2] is the mechanism that allows you to extract useful information from the museum records. The catalog divides the information in your records into useful classes or categories and provides the tool for access to this data. At one time this mechanism would have been a card file. With the advent of the computer, the concept of what a museum catalog is has been expanded, and access to both the records and the collection has been greatly extended. Despite this, the card catalog survives in many museums—some are even generated by computer. Regardless of the radically different media used in storing catalogs, there is not a lot of difference among them in the type of data stored. It is difficult to discuss paper and electronic methods separately, so I'm going to discuss them together.

The term "catalog" comes from the ancient Greek (*katalogos*) and means to count down, with the idea of counting completely. The first catalogs, as we know them, were developed in the Hellenistic period in the famous library at Alexandria. One of the interesting concepts was developed by a man named Callimachus, who arranged the catalog by author in alphabetical order—a revolutionary idea at the time. Libraries have been thinking about catalogs ever since.

The first museum ledgers that we know about were developed in the Renaissance. These listed the objects in some arbitrary order, usually the order received, in a journal. Early attempts at cataloging included keeping separate ledgers for different types of objects or for different collections.[3]

A paper catalog takes some thought to develop and a lot of work to maintain. Using the search and sort functions of a computer one can easily generate an endless number of types of catalogs.

Until relatively recently, a ledger was the preferred method of storing paper collection records. An accession ledger (whether written or electronic), accession sheets, and similar forms store almost all the information the museum has on its collection in their mass. They are useful records, and one would hardly have been considered a museum without them, but it is very difficult to extract data from them. The catalog is the easy and safe access to all this information.

It would be interesting to know who the genius was who first took the information in the accession ledger, wrote out each record on a separate piece of paper or card, and arranged these into categories to give useful information. If we knew who that person was, we should erect a statue of him or her, because he or she solved the problem of how to access the huge mass of information in the museum's records. The cards could be placed in endless combinations allowing for almost limitless searches for the information in the museum records. It was as revolutionary an idea as Callimachus arranging the library catalog alphabetically and by author in the third century BC.

The cards could also be a curse. They multiplied like flies; they were difficult to create; the files occupied a lot of space; the cards stored endless amounts of redundant data; there were multiple forms; people mixed them up, lost them, and misplaced them; and inaccurate data was safely ensconced in their depths. This is one big reason that most museums today prefer a computer database. As long as you back up the information regularly, you will probably not lose the information as easily as you could lose a card.

COMPUTERS AND CATALOGING

A computer can create any kind of catalog the mind can imagine, and it is faster and easier than any paper catalog. I would not recommend creating a paper catalog anymore. The only reasons for discussing paper catalogs at all is to discuss the type of reports (catalogs) you need. Some museums still have older paper catalog records, and a few museums still create paper catalogs from the digital records.[4]

The computer's ability to search for, sort, and index data; its ability to pull together related pieces of information; the lack of redundancy; and especially the speed make the computer the ultimate cataloging tool. One big advantage of the computer is that you need few, if any, forms. Instead of having information stored on a number of pieces of paper, and these in a number of places, the computer can store the information in one place to which access is a lot faster and easier. Inaccurate information is even more of a problem in a computer than in a card file, but the computer can often identify some of its own errors.

I do not use a card catalog anymore. I can extract more useful information from my database, either on the screen or by a written report, than could be easily extracted from any card catalog.

Even with a computer, however, it is important to understand the old card catalog systems because you may have to use an old card catalog to find information about your collection. A card might be considered an analog while a computer is digital. With a computer, you usually can see only one record at a time, but with the card catalog you could spread the cards out and look at several. When the computer is down, the card catalog or the accession file are good backups. When you are doing an inventory, the old card catalog may help you identify "found in collections" items.

While most museums do not use a card catalog any more there may be some reasons for a small museum to use one. If there is limited access to the computer, the card catalog may be a supplement to the computer, allowing for more people to have access at one time. If the collection is small, a card catalog may be easier to use than some database systems. A card catalog can provide safe public access to the records. Finally, some people are more comfortable with paper records than electronic ones.

However, if the collection is large, is constantly growing, or is audited frequently; the records are being updated; or one needs to make sophisticated searches, a computer data bank will be a lot more useful than a paper catalog. If you have a large collection, you may wish to consider if you want to have a paper catalog at all.

For the most part, the computer records have replaced the paper catalog cards. However, it helps to be familiar with them in case you need to search them for information that is not in the computer.

CATALOGING INVOLVES TWO DIFFERENT CONCEPTS

Considering the time people spend cataloging a museum collection, the definition of the act of cataloging is rather vague and there is no agreement on the meaning. There are actually several different processes that are called cataloging. They mainly fall into two classes:

1. The creation of the catalog by extracting data from your records and presenting it in some useful format.
2. The updating of the information in the collection records. Every generation of professionals that works with the collection expands the museum's knowledge about the collection. If this new understanding of the collection is written into the permanent records, it will destroy primary data. Therefore, the new information is written into the catalog. Often a completely new catalog record is created and then becomes the record of choice. When people talk about cataloging, they are usually talking about this updating process.

When you enter new data into a catalog, you may be destroying some of the old information. This old information may be valuable. To get around this problem, the museum should archive the old paper records or periodically archive a copy of its computer records. For computer records, it is important to back up the information regularly. The more active collections should have this data backed up monthly or weekly at a minimum.

WHAT DOES THE CATALOG TELL YOU?

What does a catalog tell you? That depends on what you need to know. Some questions can be fairly obscure, such as "What objects are there, and where are they located, which tell me something about the Industrial Revolution in Hero County?" Some questions are fairly simple, such as "Where are all the Windsor chairs?" Others are more complicated, such as "Is there a relationship between tapered legs and lipped drawers on tables made in Hero County before 1810?" Even a paper catalog can give you this information, though it may be harder to dig it out than it would be from a computer.

CLASSIFICATION

No catalog system will work well unless there is at least one constant used to classify the objects. The reason for this is that the constant gives you the ability to classify the whole file in some rational order. Using a constant, you can deal with the collection as a whole. Different disciplines use different classification criteria:

- Art museums use the artist, but also the period, medium, or genre.
- Natural history museums use a taxonomy based on a system first developed by Linnaeus (Karl Linné, 1707–1778).
- Earth science museums use geological epochs or chemical composition.
- History museums, until the 1970s, did not have a classification system.

The favored classifications in history museums for many years included such things as the material of which the object was made (such as "silver"), or broad topical classes ("tools"), or style ("Hepplewhite"), or, in large museums, the departments that were responsible for the collections ("Social History").

It was not until Robert Chenhall created his system in the 1970s that the idea of a systematic catalog in a history museum came about.[5] The system would be a standard taxonomy common across the whole history field and useful to anyone. To a great extent, Chenhall's dream of a systematic classification system has been widely adopted by the museum field. I will refer to the newest edition as *Nomenclature*. This system of classification arranges objects by their use and has simple naming conventions. By using *Nomenclature*, you can arrange your collection in a meaningful order that is understandable by any rational person.

The reason for using a widely accepted classification system is that it is readily understandable by many people in the museum field. A new curator, or a visiting scholar, will be able to understand your system with little instruction.

Besides, *Nomenclature* is fairly simple. If the museum develops its own classification system, it may be a lot harder to learn and may not be consistent over many changes of staff.

There are new systems that challenge the concept that you need a constant for a registration system. The cry is to let the computer make its own classification. If there is the right kind of data, many systems can do just that. Please note that numbering systems are not a classification system even though you can arrange your system by number. It is just a method of registering each object.

HOW *NOMENCLATURE* WORKS

Nomenclature classifies a collection based on how the objects are used. It has the terms arranged in a taxonomy.[6]

If you know a bit about furniture, you might describe a typical large case piece as a Kass, a Schrank, a wardrobe, a press, an armoire, or whatever. Even if the catalog entries bearing these terms were all filed under "wardrobe," this is bound to cause confusion. A person from the part of the country I come from will call a certain iron cooking utensil a "skillet," while someone from another part of the country might call it a "frying pan." Both terms are correct. Do you drive a car or an automobile? The number of synonyms does not matter in speaking or writing but does when you are classifying your collection. *Nomenclature* uses only one term for each object. Furthermore, these terms are arranged in broad families based on their use. This allows you to find records quickly. Unlike many of the old classification systems, certain types of objects could appear in every one of *Nomenclature*'s families. Most trades or skills use a hammer. These hammers are each filed separately under their use, while in the old days they would all be filed together under "hammers."

Nomenclature systemizes the naming of terms we use in identifying manmade objects. The system is not particularly difficult to adopt, even for a small museum. You have to recognize that Chenhall created not only a list of approved terms but also a whole system of classification of objects for history museums.

As an example you may have five common bench planes: a smoothing plane, a jack plane, a fore plane, a jointer, and a long jointer. Filed alphabetically by these names they would be scattered in several places in the catalog:

Fore plane (in the Fs)

Jack plane (in the Js)

Jointer plane (in the Js)

Long jointer (in the Ls)

Smoothing plane (in the Ss)

This would make searches difficult, at best, as you would have to know exactly what you were looking for in order to find it. However, if you followed the principles in *Nomenclature* and treated the noun as a genus (class) and the modifier as a species (type), you would have them arranged thusly:

plane, fore

plane, jack

plane, jointer

plane, long jointer

plane, smoothing

If you use Chenhall's families, these tools would be filed under a family name of "Tools and Equipment for Materials, Woodworking," so you would always be able to find them in one particular place, so long as you knew their use.

It is true that the nature of the English language causes a few problems. Such objects as teaspoon ("spoon, tea") or a football ("ball, foot") will not neatly arrange themselves. There are alternate spellings that create a consistency problem. In the worst cases, you can use a cross-reference.

Unless you have an unusually complex system I do not think you need a lexicon—that is, a dictionary, a list of terms. If you do need a lexicon, then setting one up is simple. If you have a computer, you can generate a word list that will be the basis of a lexicon. Some systems will do word counts for you that will simplify the process. It is a little more difficult with a manual system. A relatively easy way for a museum to set up a lexicon with a manual system is to go through your catalog. Each term should be compared against *Nomenclature*'s list. If it is not on the list, then you have to create a term. *Nomenclature* explains how to do this. Enter the term on a card. This will help with later descriptions. You need to enter each term only once. In a collection of fifteen thousand items I used only about five hundred terms while *Nomenclature* lists more than five thousand.

Some museums have a separate listing of their catalog headings. These listings often became part of the registrar's manual or the operating procedures of the museum. That helps avoid duplication, is especially handy with a large staff, and may be necessary if the museum is developing a nomenclature. However, I really do not think a small museum has to worry about listing its headings separately. That is just one more thing to take care of, and if you really want to know what your headings are, you can look in the catalog drawer or in your computer's data bank. *Nomenclature* supplies a set of ready-made headings for you.

If you color-code your dividing cards, so that you can tell the main heading from the subheadings, it is easier. Cards are filed by accession number inside each classification.

ALTERNATES TO *NOMENCLATURE*

There is an alternate to *Nomenclature*. There are such things as "authority lists" or "vocabularies."[7] These are lists of approved terms. *The Art and Architecture Thesaurus* is the best known of this type in the museum field. Most have several approved terms for every type of object. Indeed, several have every possible term. Most authority lists are for specific types of collections. They are too large and cumbersome for small museums, approaching the size of unabridged dictionaries in some cases. Unless you have an exceedingly unusual collection, I would not recommend them for small museums.

WHAT CATALOGS DO YOU NEED?

If you follow the concepts in this book, basic records of your museum registration system that we have developed so far will consist of:

- Transfer of title document consisting of a gift agreement, bill of sale, or some other document transferring title to the museum.
- Accessions register containing the accession number, brief description of what is in the accession, the source, the method of acquisition, and the date of acquisition. The ledger may serve as this document.
- Accession record on each object in the accession. This would include all the information you have on an object. Paper records should be bound into an accession ledger or book.
- Accession file consisting of correspondence, research notes, documents, and other records of each accession in a file.

You will need all these records if you are writing them into a bound ledger with a quill pen, or typing them into a paperless system on a computer, or every technique in between. I am convinced that I could get a small museum accredited by the American Alliance of Museums with no more collection records than these primary records. The catalog is the device that not only protects these records but also gives you access to them.

I am going to discuss manual (or paper) catalogs separately from ones generated by the computer.

Manual Catalogs

Most museums have moved away from a manual catalog system because of the availability of computers and database programs. However, it is important to understand these manual systems, such as card catalogs, and how they are made so that you can use them to research your collection. Often, there is information in these old records that has not made it into the database. It is important to understand how these records are created and used so that you can go back and research them efficiently. Also, in some small, volunteer-run institutions, a manual system may still be in use. If you are going to be the person moving the records to a computer database, you will need to have an understanding of these systems.

It is impossible to advise anyone on what catalogs you may find in a museum without seeing the museum and its records. I suggest searching for the following types of catalogs, as they are the most common in old museum records.

Main Entry Catalog

A main entry is the card or record upon which any other type of record in the catalog is modeled. In fact, the easiest way to make other catalogs is to copy the main entry card. (See textbox 6.1.) This card contains the information for most searches. The name of the museum is at the bottom so that more useful information can be accessed from the top.

TEXTBOX 6.1

MAIN ENTRY CARD

Object: Plate, Dinner	**Acc. No.:** 1952.2.1
Classification: 04 Food Service	
Source: Ivy Propan	
Location: 101	
Material: Ceramic	**Size:** 11.375 dia. × 0.875
Maker: Clews	**Place Made:** England
Date: ca. 1830	**Association:** Lafayette

Description:
Flat bowl with curving sides; marley curves up; lip faintly scalloped; foot ring; underglaze blue transfer of lading of Lafayette over white ground; on bottom is stamp between two circles, "Clews Warranted safe [illegible]"; and, in underglaze blue, "The Landing of Lafayette at Castle Garden New York 16 August 1824."

HERO COUNTY HISTORICAL MUSEUM

The main entry card contains most of the catalog information. Just what the catalog information is, is up to the person who created the system, but it would logically consist of the accession number, the source, and the descriptive information. This type of information is discussed in chapter 4. If there is only one catalog, it will most likely be a main entry card, and all of the cards will be arranged by *Nomenclature*'s principles. With these systems, you can answer such complicated questions as "What furniture do we have that was made in Hero County before 1800 by known cabinetmakers?" When you can answer that kind of sophisticated question from the entry catalog, you have to question the wisdom of having several.[8]

If there are photographs of the collection, they are often on the main entry card. It saves looking in another catalog for an image.

The Source or Donor Catalog

Another catalog that was necessary to operate the museum was the donor or source catalog. Keep in mind that the sources of funds for purchases are also donors. These systems may have a list of vendors as well. Museums that depend on donors for most of their accessions will usually find such a file. These files were easy to make up, since all you needed was a brief description of the accession and the accession number. All the other information is in the accession records. A donor card might look like those shown in textboxes 6.2, 6.3, and 6.4.

TEXTBOX 6.2

SINGLE-NUMBER DONOR CARD

Sarah Bellum

28-132
34'5 -362
421-447
1002

TEXTBOX 6.3

TWO-NUMBER DONOR CARD

Sarah Bellum

1956.3-.9
1932.32-.33
1975.12-.14

TEXTBOX 6.4

THREE-NUMBER DONOR CARD

Truck, Mr. and Mrs. Mack (Dorothy)

1956.36.1-.36 Toolbox and tools
1962.33.1-20 Garments, papers, photos
1975.5.1-.9 Dining room table and chairs

In the single number (textbox 6.2) and two-number systems (textbox 6.3), you would have to enter a range of numbers that cover the accession. These systems should only have one card for each source.

Tracking Location

Because good museum practice requires that you place your hands on any object at short notice, one of the things you need to know is the location of each object in your museum. The standard method was to write the location in pencil on your main entry card. Every time you would move the object, you would change the location on the card. This can be a complicated and time-consuming task.

Another method was to have a card on each object filed by location. When you would move the object, you would move the card. This would have been handy when someone asked you about the spittoon in the main room or when doing inventories. The problems associated with a separate card file for location is that you cannot find the location from the main entry catalog, so often you will find the location in pencil on that card as well, which means the location was kept in two places. It also means that sometimes the location is accurate on one card but was not updated on the other. One of the advantages of a computerized registration system is its ability to easily generate a location catalog.

Partly to resolve these problems, and partly because you cannot write a location on a computer record in pencil, a system of having objects "live" at one location was developed. The object was assigned to a permanent location in where it "lives." The only time the location was tracked is when the object is moved. You will still see this system in computer records where you have a "permanent location" and a "temporary location."

You will also find that some museums kept binders with cards or object lists in rooms in a small museum to help answer questions about the collections. If these binders still exist, they can be useful to figure out the "found in collections" items that you will come across during an inventory. Some of these records are computer-generated reports with the objects arranged by location.

An exhibit catalog is a permanent record of what was in the exhibit. It can be in any form, but it may be best typed up on sheets and filed with the other material on the exhibit. The simplest way to make one was to Xerox the cards onto a sheet of paper. Now we can generate a complete catalog of the items in each exhibit from our databases. If a question comes up, I can then find all the information I need in one place. In the old days, we Xeroxed the catalog cards of objects on exhibit.

TEXTBOX 6.5

ASSOCIATION CARD

Gomorra Pool Hall
Main Street, Hero (1929–1979)

1962.29.27	Pool cue
1970.2.3	Snooker championship cup
1977.38.1	Photo of "gang" at hall
1976.99.8	Scrapbook of trial

Cross Ref.: Lott, G. D. (owner); Main Street; Recreation; Billiard Halls

HERO COUNTY HISTORICAL MUSEUM

ASSOCIATION CATALOG

Part of the information that gives an object value is its association with people, places, or events. The association is often more important than the object. A silk hat is a silk hat, but if it had been Abraham Lincoln's silk hat . . . ! An object may have a manufacturer's name on it or may be associated with a particular event, such as the Civil War, or with a particular place, such as a local reform school. An easy way to access the knowledge of this association can be a valuable aid in research and developing exhibits. An association catalog was one way to help you do this. (See textbox 6.5.)

Association cards are somewhat like donor cards, but they would have the title of the object as well as the name of the association and the accession numbers. A typical example would look like textbox 6.5.

When you would have planned to make an exhibit on Main Street or on recreation in Hero, or on pool halls, or on G. D. Lott, you would have looked up the information in your association file. These files helped you cross-reference the collection and would assist in finding collections related to the same topics that were donated at different times and sometimes by different people.

IMAGES OF THE COLLECTION

Photographs and Digital Images

The trite old saying about a picture being worth a thousand words is particularly true of a registration system. An image of the object makes any description much clearer and can help greatly in identifying objects. Images are also useful in showing condition.[9] I would not recommend using film as digital images have pretty much replaced it.

Equipment to take good images of the collection is readily available, inexpensive, and easy to operate. If the museum staff does not have the expertise or time, there are many people who do who can be asked to take images as a volunteer activity. It is best to take an image of each object in the collection as it is accessioned. If that is impossible, try to take an image of the more important objects.

The purpose of the photograph is for identification. Although a good photograph is desirable, you are not turning out a work of art. The picture's main purpose is identification. Each object should be photographed individually, as it is almost impossible to photograph a group of objects well enough for identification purposes. If you are still using film, a contact print should be made of the negative from each frame and the negative fastened in a sleeve to the back. These sleeves are readily available from archive supply houses.

If you have a film archive of your collection, one way to have a catalog is to have a print made of each object and file them in accession number order. More often, though, the field is moving to scanning these images or taking new digital images. However, if you do make a print file, the information you need can be printed on the back. If you have a rubber stamp made containing the information you need, the job becomes much easier. With a computer, you can generate a label that will do the same thing. The negative is more important than the prints, so keeping track of them is important. You should never use the stamp or label on historic photographs or documents. You will find that a digital image is a much easier way, and it is cheaper and easier to find than film is these days.

There are a number of ways to store photographs electronically. These systems are very valuable, as you can bring up the image with the catalog record. The technology is evolving rapidly and is getting cheaper and cheaper to use. These electronically stored records can be brought up with the catalog records, and give your audience access to the collection without having to handle the objects.[10]

Remember, electronically stored data does not have an infinite shelf life—in fact, it is relatively short—while a properly made and stored photograph on archive-quality paper has a long life. It may be very difficult to convert an image from one format to another, although a majority of programs will read most imaging conventions. Media storage is also constantly evolving. Compact discs (CDs) were commonly used just a few years ago; however, it is now difficult to find a computer with a CD or DVD drive. Many of the technologies we use are short lived, and hardware and software to read the digitally stored records may be short lived. This is why it is a good idea to print that photograph for your records.

Some people also use movie cameras, or camcorders, to make a record of their collections. This has the benefit that you can dictate information about the collection as you are recording it. Like the digital photographs, these records will be dependent on you having software that can read your file.

CARD CATALOGS

If you are still making card catalogs, you can still get cards from library suppliers or make your own out of cardstock. These cards are getting harder to find because fewer museums and libraries are making physical card catalogs. If you do make a card catalog, I would recommend a larger card, such as four by six inches, which holds a great deal more information than the standard three-by-five-inch card. However, they are harder to find in the right cardstock, and it is difficult to get file cabinets for them. The ubiquitous three-by-five-inch card is easier to find, and the file cabinets for them are obtainable from several sources. Since card file cabinets get a great deal of use, in institutions with manual systems, the cabinet should be of good quality.

In the days when every card had to be typed by hand, typing them on good cardstock made sense because you expected the card to last forever. Now that even the smallest museum will have access to a computer, a cheaper stock may be used. As records are updated the old cards are thrown out and new ones generated. Some museums generate a whole new card catalog periodically and archive the old one.

Each object should have its own card, except in cases of pairs or small sets of less than, say, five items.

Even a small museum will need a large number of cards. Printing a form on them can be expensive. For this reason, I am recommending that only one type of card be printed, although it is possible to place all the information on a blank card. This is the main entry card. You can use the same card form for several different types of catalogs.

Typing or printing catalog cards is a real chore. Any step you can take to reduce the work is worth the effort. It is a good idea to arrange the data on the worksheet (see appendix A) in the same order that it is typed on the cards. This will promote accuracy as well as speed up the process.

MANUAL CATALOGS WITHOUT CARDS

There are catalogs without cards. One kind is a computer catalog. Some museums have very static collections or static exhibits. In such instances, it is often easier to list the information on sheets of paper. These "page catalogs" are kept in file drawers or loose-leaf binders and can easily be copied on any office copier. The big disadvantage is that a change in any item affects the whole catalog.

I have discussed paper catalogs chiefly in terms of cards. This is because they were the most common form of catalog system that was made and the ones you are most likely to find in your old records. The advantages of cards over lists on paper led to this common decision. Two reasons are that cards could be easily shuffled and a change on one card did not affect the whole list.

COMPUTER CATALOGS

You need the same kind of information from a computer catalog that you need from a card file; it is just stored differently. There should be some assurance that your program can extract the information you want and present it in some usable format on both screen and paper. These reports are substitutes for the old paper catalogs. Most data management programs can be made to configure almost any kind of report using the data in its database.

You need to be able to access the information you need. You might wish to generate a list of all the silver in storage, which would make searches a lot easier. You might have the list sorted by accession number, location, donor, and title. These will do very well as catalogs. You have an advantage in that you can often take a printout of the whole catalog (or the laptop or tablet) with you when you go into collections storage. The corrected data can be entered into your computer to keep the master record complete and accurate. However, if you want them, the computer can just as easily generate your catalog cards.

Again, size of the collection plays a part in whether you generate paper catalogs from the computer. It is much easier for a small collection to have a printout than a large museum. Generating 3,000 cards with the typical office printer may be more than a day's work; generating 100,000 pages may take more than a month. Even simple reports, where each record takes up only one line, can be quite extensive. A complete report of one line of data for each record of a collection of 10,000 objects might well take up over 200 pages. Still, that is less than the seven or so drawers a card catalog might take. Most museums with a database generate reports for a specific task, such as an inventory, and use the computer for cataloging.

USING THE DESCRIPTION AS A CATALOG DEVICE

A computer gives you a big advantage in its ability to search out information anywhere in the record. If you use the same standards of *Nomenclature* in the material you put in the description field, rather than in a number of fields, you can cut the amount of work necessary to enter and maintain data and can extract a lot more information. From this you can easily pick out such things as the gouges with inside bevels, or what percentage has sockets rather than tangs. If you have a similar worksheet for furniture, you can easily pick up all the case pieces with lipped drawers. I was once asked for all the tables with an outside taper on the legs, an easy question to answer if the information is there.

INVENTORIES

The inventory is used to check the accuracy of the information you have on each object, its condition, and its location.[11] Catalogs will stay up to date only if there is a periodic inventory. The ideal is to inventory your collection once a year. This may be beyond the capabilities of the museum, particularly if there is a small staff, but if you do a percentage of the collection each year, you will have a completed inventory in a few years. For example, if you inventory a third of the collection a year, then it will be completed in three years. I would bet that any museum that has not been inventoried in the last three to five years has numerous problems with its registration system.

There is the problem of the large collection. A collection of 10,000 may take several teams a few weeks to inventory, but what about a collection with 100,000 objects? In this situation, it may be necessary to take a "spot" inventory. This inventory only looks at a small portion of the collection to see if there are problems. You might take 1,000 records at random and see if you can find the objects and if their records are up to date. Then pick 1,000 items objects from several areas and examine their records. If there are few problems, this will give you an idea of the state of the collection, but it is not a complete inventory and any problems lurking below the surface may stay undiscovered for a long while.

For manual systems, many museums inventory by making a list of the objects as they are found and checking that list against the records. That list becomes an accurate record of the state of the collection at that particular time. There is, however, a lot of cross-checking of records.

You may find it easier to take one of your card catalogs and move the card for each object you find to the *found* file as you go through the collection. This method does not produce a list, so you must make one from the completed catalog. I use this method and create a list in accession number order as I go along.

It is a lot easier inventorying a collection with a computer database. You generate a list of the objects by location and check them off as you find them, or you can take the computer with you as you work, if it is small enough.

It is important with inventories that you end up with some list showing the state of the collection at that particular point in time. This list should be archived.

Certain technologies have helped speed up the inventory process in some museums. Laptops and tablets with wireless capabilities make it possible for staff to take the museum's catalog to storage to inventory the objects. Bar code and RFID technologies can help automate the process and limit the number of transcription errors and handling. These technologies are becoming cheaper and cheaper and are now in use in many museums. The challenge with bar codes and RFID tags is where to put them.[12] The museum has not yet solved the problem of placing the bar codes and RFID tags directly on the object. There are safe ways of attaching them using paper tags or by putting them on the storage mount or container.

An inventory requires a large commitment on the part of the museum. Make sure you can complete it before you start. One of the curses badly registered systems have is all of the incomplete inventories with which one has to deal.

ACCESS

How much of the museum's records are public documents is a question you should consider carefully. Most museums do not consider any of the registration records public information. In most cases access is restricted to only a few of the museum personnel. This practice is a sensible one. Any data made public is carefully edited before release. Remember, labels, exhibit catalogs, education programs, and similar published information are public releases of information about your catalog.

Many museums have *portions* of their catalog easily available to the public through a computer, or even have a catalog on the Internet. This gives the public access without endangering the records or revealing any secrets.

If the museum catalog is considered a public document, there should be some restrictions on how it is used by the public. Locations and valuations should be privileged information. Privacy laws restrict the use of donors' names and addresses. Knowledge about the size of certain holdings may make you a juicy target for thieves.

Catalogs bring up the question of access, not only to the museum records but also to the collection. The museum has to grant everyone equal access to the collection. This does not mean that you have to admit everyone at any time they want, but you have to let people under similar circumstances have *equal* access. It is a good idea to develop a policy on access to the records and the collection. Access can be limited to legitimate research goals and a need-to-know basis. The type of examination can be restricted to certain times and methods of examination. You can forbid the handling of the object, if that is in the best interest.[13]

The examination of records can be limited to the catalog. You can keep certain information confidential, such as the value, location, and donor's name. Government-run museums may come under so-called sunshine laws, by which they have to grant everyone access to the collection. That access does not necessarily have to be the records. You may have to give some person a list of your Chinese teapots, but that doesn't mean you need to give them the whole catalog. Even in these cases, certain knowledge, such as donors' names and the location and value of objects can be restricted, and need-to-know questions arise. Your lawyer can advise you on this issue.

I have placed a clause on access to the collection in the policy manuals in the appendix.

WHAT NOT TO DO AND WHEN NOT TO DO IT

A mistake people often make about the catalog is to confuse it with the accession records. It is tempting to type all the accession records, neatly file them in some fashion, and say you have a catalog. It is equally easy to take a card from the card catalog or paper file and use it or misplace it; then you have lost one of the primary records of the museum. This was true of all the problem collections with which I have dealt. If you are going to have a manual catalog, keep it separate from primary records. The paper catalogs get used and will eventually have to be replaced, computer catalogs can be accessed through your database system, but the primary accession records should last forever.

I realize that if the museum uses a ledger as its catalog, it could eventually wear it out. I recommend in this case that the museum make a copy and use the copy instead of the original. In fact, you should copy any primary record that is going to be consulted frequently and use the copy as the working document.

There is a trick to cataloging. The trick is to do it right the first time. It is a common mistake when cataloging to start off on the wrong foot, do half a job, drop it, come back later, and start again. The result is a mess. It is better to decide, at the beginning, what you really want to do, begin it carefully, and complete one section before going on to the next. This holds true whether it is a manual system or a computerized system.

CONCLUSION

Cataloging is as much a process as it is a device. The process is a constant updating of the data of the collection. This is the way we pass our knowledge on to the next set of curators. There should be a commitment on the part of the museum to updating the catalog.

The test of any catalog is not whether you can use it but whether anyone else can. It should be arranged so it makes sense to anyone. Good cataloging consists of:

1. Examining every object and every record and creating an accurate description.
2. Developing a usable set of categories for searches you will actually make.
3. Developing a program to keep the data up to date.

For paper catalogs the purpose of cataloging is to arrange your records in usable categories. It is easier to shuffle cards than objects. Museum personnel should decide what information will be needed from the catalog and then divide the catalog into those units. There may be other methods of cataloging available that do not use cards. The museum must be careful not to create a catalog monster that will eat up all the professional staff's time. As I said before, these paper systems are disappearing and being replaced by computer systems. However, it is still important to know how these systems were created so that you can go back and use the paper records at your institution. There may be some hidden gem of information that did not make it to the database, and the only way you may find it is by familiarizing yourself with the old system.

A computerized catalog should quickly and easily provide the information you need in a useable form. Like the card catalog, the system should be usable to any intelligent person, though he or she may have to learn the idiosyncrasies of the program first, and questions of data security may arise. Don't make the mistake of thinking that everything is in the database. You should check other sources, such as the paper records, when updating your computer catalog.

NOTES

1. AAM, *Peer Review Manual*, F8.

2. For a look at how librarian would handle museum cataloging, see Murtha Baca, Patricia Harping, Elisa Lanzi, Linda McRae, and Ann Whiteside, *Cataloging Cultural Objects: A Guide to Describing Cultural Objects and Their Images* (Chicago: American Library Association, 2006). The system Baca and colleagues propose is too extensive for most museums. The term "catalogue" may be correctly spelled as either "catalog" or "catalogue."

3. The question of who had the first museum registration system is moot. Herodotus implies, in the fifth century BC, that there were catalogs for the collections in several treasuries (that held historical collections) at Delphi and in Mesopotamia. This information may have been oral, but at least the priests could account for their collections and pass this knowledge on to others. Some of the information was written directly on the object. This is a method frowned on today, but one must say that it would be hard to lose your catalog. The concept of a collection ledger was developed in the Hellenistic times (350–0 BC). There are collection ledgers referred to for the Renaissance collections. For a survey, see Geoffery D. Lewis, "Collections, Collectors and Museums: A Brief World Survey," in John M. A. Thompson et al., eds., *Manual of Curatorship: A Guide to Museum Practice* (London: Butterworths, 1984).

4. Compare Kitty Longstreth-Brown, "Records Management: Manual Systems," in Buck and Gilmore, *MRM5*, 155–60, and Suzanne Quigley, "Records Management: Computerized Systems," in Buck and Gilmore, *MRM5*, 161–83.

5. *Nomenclature* is still in print and is on its fourth edition. It is interesting, but Chenhall's work, originally meant to aid in computerization of collections, has proven even more useful with manual records.

6. A taxonomy is the classification of a something into a natural arrangement. The list itself is a taxis. "Lexicon," "nomenclature," and "dictionary" are more or less interchangeable terms.

7. Elisa Lanzi et al., *Introduction to Vocabularies: Enhancing Access to Cultural Heritage Information* (Los Angeles: J. Paul Getty Trust, 1998).

8. The reason for placing the name of the museum at the bottom of the card in the example is that it will identify the museum, while the important information is at the top. This is not required, and many museums prefer to have the institution's name at the top of the card.

9. Marie Demeroukas, "Condition Reporting," in Buck and Gilmore, *MRM5*, 223–32.

10. Jill Marie Koelling, *Digital Imaging: A Practical Approach* (Walnut Creek, CA: AltaMira Press, 2004); Christie Stephenson and Patricia McClung, eds., *Delivering Digital Images: Cultural Heritage Resources for Education* (Los Angeles: The Getty Institute, 1998).

11. Maureen McCormick, "Inventory," in Buck and Gilmore, *MRM5*, 300–6.

12. Catherine Zwiesler, "Barcoding," *Spectra* 23, no. 1 (Fall 1995), 18–20, discusses use of bar codes at the National Museum of Natural History. *Spectra* was the newsletter of the Museum Computer Network. See also Gabor R. Racz, "Improving Collections Maintenance through Innovation: Bar-Code Labeling to Track Specimens in the Processing Stream," *Collections* 1, no. 3 (February 2005), 227–41; Suzanne Fishman-Armstrong and Deborah Rose Van Horn, "Considerations for Implementing a Bar Code System in a Museum," *Collections* 4, no. 4 (Fall 2008), 333–48.

13. Access to the museum collection and the records has not been a very big issue until recently. It is the kind of situation people worry about before it happens. However, it is good to be prepared.

Loans

Unless the exhibits and the collection are very static, a museum will lend and borrow objects. The museum will find that its collection is never complete enough to make up every exhibit. It is a good museum practice and good public relations to have exhibits of items from the community. Other museums and organizations will want to tap your resources. Items are often lent or borrowed for purposes of study or conservation. The sophisticated handling of loans is part of the registration process. Like any other part of the registration process, the museum should decide how deeply it wants to get into loans and create the policy to do this, and the procedures will develop out of this.[1]

LOAN POLICY

Many problems with loans will never occur if the museum has a strong policy on loans. The policy should ensure that:

- The loan furthers the purpose of the museum. If your statement of purpose declares that the museum wishes "to encourage the preservation and study of Hero County history," then the loan should do just that.
- The object will be cared for properly while on loan.
- The registration system can track the object over the whole period of the loan, even if that is several years!

Every loan should be tested against these conditions. There are examples of such policies in appendixes B and C.

There is something of a difference between things a museum borrows and things it lends, so we are going to discuss these separately. As in any other contractual relationship between a museum and second parties, the loan policies, the loan form, and the types of liability assumed should be gone over carefully with a lawyer before the museum becomes involved in loans.

LOANS FROM THE MUSEUM

When a museum lends items out from its collection, it is very simple. The museum owns the object lent and can set its own conditions. The museum can have absolute control over how the object is used. Criteria for conditions for loans from the museum are listed below and in appendix A-9.

LOANS TO THE MUSEUM

You are on slightly different ground when you borrow something than when you lend an object. When you lend, the object involved is your property, and you can set the conditions. When you borrow an item, it is not your property, you must follow the owner's wishes, and you take on a liability. You are obligated to return the loan in the same condition in which you received it. You are responsible for it as long as you have it. If the owner does not show up to reclaim it, you are still responsible for it. If the lender appears thirty-three years later, as happened to me once, you are still responsible. Therefore, it is a very good idea to borrow only for specific purposes, such as display, and for a specific time period, and return things as soon as possible.

On a loan to the museum, you must usually provide the protection, shipping costs, and insurance. Most museums agree to protect the item as if it were their own and to carry fine arts insurance. The owner may want to set other conditions, and these should be stated on the form. Criteria for conditions for a loan to the museum are below and in appendix A-10.

WHOSE LOAN PROCEDURES WILL APPLY?

As a practical matter, there should be only one loan agreement for a loan. On loans between museums, the lending institution will have the upper hand in negotiations, and it will almost always be its procedure and forms. This can be pretty tricky when museums vary widely in operating procedures. On third-party loans, such as loans for traveling exhibits, the policies of the originating museum will probably apply. Your loan form for loans to your museum is for people who normally do not have their own form, such as individuals and private companies.

CONDITIONS OF LOANS

The general conditions affecting every loan should be printed on the loan form and discussed with the other parties. If there will be special conditions that are not on the loan form, these should then be made a written part of the loan documents. Before the object is moved the loan form should be signed by all parties.

Whether the loan is from or to the museum, certain conditions arise that should be accounted for in the museum's policy and loan arrangements.

What Is Actually Being Borrowed?

The loan form should state exactly what is being borrowed, listing every item. On loans from your museum, your accession records are very handy as you can place the accession number and a description from your records on the loan form. On loans to the museum, you may have to go to the lending person or agency and make an exact description of what is borrowed and do a condition report.

The description of the object should be good enough to identify it in court. The museum's description of its own objects should do that. If the description of a borrowed item is not good enough, you will have to make a new one. When borrowing from a private person you should go over the description and make sure the lender agrees with your description, particularly of condition.

The condition report can be separate from your form, but I would encourage you to do them for every incoming and outgoing item. It not only helps identify the piece but also helps with insurance claims if there is any damage.[2]

The Exact Purpose of the Loan

The purpose of the loan should be stated on the form. If you lend a copper pot for exhibition, you do not want to see it used for cooking. It is best for the museum to have a policy on limiting loans to certain specific purposes. Many museums simplify the process by developing a policy that they will only borrow objects for exhibition in the museum and only lend objects to other museums for the same purpose. Museums with a local following may find it expedient to lend to community organizations that are able to take care of the object. In addition, there should be some way to lend objects for conservation or study.

How the Object Is to Be Cared for and Handled While on Loan

It is very important to have an understanding of exactly how the object is to be handled while on exhibit. That means, if it is to be exhibited only, how much, if any, access will anyone have to it during the loan? Additionally, what happens before it reaches its final destination? Is the janitor going to unpack it or the curator? Where is it going to be stored en route? Who is going to handle it while on exhibit and how? Who is going to pack it when the loan period is up? These are typical but important considerations.

Normally, the borrowers' care of the object is limited to simple dusting, although that may not be allowed for certain objects. The other party should notify the lender of any change in the condition of the object and be forbidden to make repairs in case of damage. How the object is to be cased, lighted, protected, and other environmental concerns are all conditions that should be agreed upon in advance.

If the object requires special handling, should not be in harsh light, must be in controlled humidity, needs special security, and so forth, these conditions should be gone over step by step with the borrower before the loan is made. It is a good idea to go over all the provisions of the loan before the loan form is signed.

An Assessment of the Object's Condition and Ability to Travel and Withstand the Conditions It Will Be Under During the Loan

Any details of condition should be noted before the object is sent out. The condition should be the same when it is brought back. You should have a condition report (see appendix A) on each object in the loan, whether from or to the museum, and have both parties agree to the statements on this form. You may need two condition reports or have to update the original: once when the object is lent, and once when the object is returned. If you are borrowing an object, and there is no condition report by the lender, then that should be noted. In these cases, you should make a condition report at the time of receipt, and that will serve as the condition report of record. Otherwise, the borrower may claim that you caused old damage.

Condition reports should be made out not only when the object is loaned but also whenever it is examined. Ideally, there should be at least one condition report on each object in the collection. As the object is monitored, you can amend the form.

The condition of the building that houses the object is also a consideration. Many museums have a facility report that they use for loans to other agencies. There is a standard form developed by the Registrars Committee of the American Alliance of Museums called the General Facilities Report.[3] Filling out the facilities report can be a time-consuming and daunting process for some small institutions. However, it has to be filled out only once, and then it can be easily altered and used with any other loan.

An object may be in good enough condition to be exhibited in one place but too fragile to be exhibited in another. An assessment of the object's ability to travel is an important part of the loan process. If the other party really has to have this object, it is an occasional practice for them to pay for the conservation necessary (or at least share the cost) to have the object travel.

Method of Packing and Crating

How the object is to be packed for shipping and who will do it are important questions. For many objects, packing as for a typical move of household goods is not good enough, and for most objects, specialized packing or crating will usually be required, and even climate control may be necessary. Unpacking is a concern at both ends of the deal, when it goes out and when it comes back. How this is done and who will pack and unpack should be part of the loan agreement.

Method of Transporting the Object and Who Is Responsible for the Shipment

There is a museum in western Pennsylvania where board members were expected to move objects. They once had a provision that to become a board member you had to have a pickup truck. That may work with agricultural equipment, but it will not work in most museums.

Make sure that both borrower and lender know how the object is to be transferred and know who is responsible for the transfer. Is it going to be the curator, a courier, a trucking company, a local moving company, or an expert in transporting fine arts? The borrower is usually responsible for making the arrangements and paying for the move. These conditions should be approved by every party. When lending objects, make sure the borrower will move the object with sufficient care, equipment, and personnel *both* ways.

The problem you sometimes run into in loans is where the other party will be located at the end of the loan term. If you borrow an object from a lender who is located ten miles away, then the costs and problems of the move are very clear. But what happens if the lender moves 3,000 miles away during the loan period? This situation does not apply only to individuals but can happen to museums as well. It is best to specify that the costs of the move apply to shipment only to the address on the loan form.

What happens if the owners sell or transfer the property while it is on loan is also a consideration. They should notify you in writing if this occurs. You should normally not return an object to anyone but the person who signed the loan form as the owner. If it is transferred, it is the owner's responsibility to provide proof of the transfer, not the museum's. This proof can be a will showing who inherited it, a court document (in cases of divorce), letters/receipts detailing the transfer of title, and so on.

Museums often have problems of not being able to return an object when the loan period is up. The owner, for one reason or another, is not available to take it back. The museum should require that if it cannot return the object because the owner cannot receive it, then the museum can exercise a lower standard of care or even charge rent. In some states, it is possible that the object could eventually become the museum's property by exercising the museum's rights under abandoned property law. Most museums, however, may be required to keep the property indefinitely until a legitimate owner is ready to receive it. In the case of the death of the owner, the museum may have to keep the object until the estate is settled. This can take years.

All the Locations in Which the Loan Will Be

The exact route the object is to take to its final destination, and where it will rest en route, should be agreed upon. I once had a very valuable object left untended in the middle of a mall by someone I thought was a responsible borrower. I was lucky that I happened along to rescue it.

It is best if the borrower keeps the object in his or her possession and returns it to the museum when the term of the loan is completed. Sometimes there is a reason to lend it to a third party. A good example would be a museum making a traveling exhibition from the collections of several museums. Any loan to a third party should be approved by the lender and put in to the loan form or signed off on with an addendum to the loan.

The Exact Dates of the Loan Period, Wall to Wall

The loan form should include the date that the agreement is made, the date the object is to be picked up, the dates of the exhibit (if the object is lent for that purpose), and the date it is to be returned. There should never be any confusion about loan dates.

Almost all loans are made "wall to wall." That means that the borrower is responsible for the object from the time that it is first handled to prepare it to be moved until it is returned to that same place, or one mutually agreeable to both parties. That means the borrower's responsibility begins once anyone lays his or her hands on it while it is still in the owner's building.

There are "door to door" agreements, in which the borrower is responsible for the object only after it leaves the lender's door, until it is returned there. If you do not specify that the loan is "wall to wall" in the loan agreement, then it would probably be considered "door to door."

The loan should have definite time limits. A loan to the museum should not continue for a long period of time; a year is long enough, and three years are about the maximum. Occasionally, museums borrow for longer periods of time. One should hesitate to request an unusually long time period, but sometimes there is a good reason, such as it may be the only way some rare item can be exhibited. These long-term loans should be for a period of a year and renewable from year to year. This practice will remind both parties that it is still a loan and will remind you to keep up your fine arts insurance. The number of these long-term loans should be kept to a minimum.

The Value of Each Object in the Loan

The value of the object is a very complicated thing when insurance is involved. If you have a damaged object that is worth $1,000 and the conservation costs are $1,500, who is responsible for the difference? Again, the insurance company may pay the $1,000 and then take the object for its salvage value. The owners may only get $800 or so if they keep the object. What happens if one of a set gets destroyed? Overvaluing an object to take care of some of this may not work, as the insurance company will insure only a "fair market value." Emotional value is not usually insurable. The museum should agree that it is responsible only for the declared value and make sure that value is reasonable for each object.

Each object in the loan should have its own value. This is important as damage or theft to the whole loan will practically never come up, but damage to a single piece will be an occasional occurrence. Sometimes the museum will have exhibits of items collected from the community, such as a senior citizens' art fair. It may be impossible to evaluate each object, but you can give a range of values, $X–$XXX, so that will cover the whole loan.

The museum should be careful about offering to place a value on objects lent to it. This may place the museum in the position of evaluating the object for market. If something happens and the value is incorrect, it may place the museum in a bad legal position. The owner might claim damages. If there is a problem with this, then you may have to hire an appraiser. Who pays for this is an interesting question.

The Type and Nature of the Insurance and Who Is Responsible for Paying for It

You need to have a fine arts policy. First of all, you are dealing with people who work with museums. It is cheaper than casualty insurance and is better for the time the accession is in transit. Normal casualty insurance will not work as it is interested only in salvage value.

The usual practice is for the borrower to be responsible for the insurance. It is important to have proof of insurance. There is a form any insurance agent should be able to produce called a "certificate of insurance." When borrowing make sure that the insurance is not due to expire while the object is on loan. The expiration date will usually be on the certificate of insurance. A 120-day cancellation clause is a useful thing on these certificates of insurance. In the case of objects of small value, where the borrower is well known, the museum may waive the demand for insurance. The lender really does not want the money; they want the object back in the same condition it was when you borrowed it.

The Name and Signature of the Person Responsible for the Loan

If the person borrowing the object represents the organization, he or she should be responsible enough to place his or her organization under the obligation of caring for the object.

The person who signs for the loan should be a person who is really responsible for it, not the person who is picking it up. These are often two different people. The person who picks up the object should also sign but may not be the responsible person.

This can be one of the tricky parts of loan arrangements. The organization responsible for the object may not be located at the museum, or even be in the same city (or state) as the exhibiting organization. It is important to get the name of a responsible person and the exact address of everyone involved. If there is a parent organization, it might be a good idea to find out if it knows that its satellite museum is borrowing the object. Museums may have different street addresses for the offices, the exhibit hall, and the shipping dock. Get them all.

Request for the Return of the Loan Before the Loan Period Is Up

It is not unknown for an owner to request the return of the object before the loan period is up. That may leave a big hole in your exhibit. Common practice is to allow this, but to require a thirty- or sixty-day notice before exercising this right. It is customary to have the person requesting the early return of the loan to pay for the packing and shipping fees.

Control of Intellectual Property

The intellectual property of the museum consists of such things as the images of the objects in the collection, the content and appearance of documents, the content and methods of education programs, publications, and so on. If the appearance of the building or site of the museum is part of the "signature" or "brand" of the museum, that, too, is intellectual property. Museums were pretty careless with their intellectual property rights until recently. With the advent of sophisticated communication devices this intellectual property suddenly has a real value to the museum. Steps should be made to protect it particularly while on loan.

Although the image or design of the object itself may be in the public domain, a photographic or electronic image of it may be copyrighted as will a reproduction of the object itself. Museums should control who takes these images or makes copies and what purposes they are used for. Before you allow anyone to photograph or otherwise copy anything in the museum, you should restrict the use of it to a certain time period and to certain uses ("A one-time use in a book on left-handed monkey wrenches"). While the object is on loan to another institution, you may want to restrict the right to photograph the object only to record-keeping purposes or a catalog.

The new forms of digital media are so sophisticated that the museum has to make a decision or you can lose all control over the image of an object in your collection. This decision is whether to restrict the use of the photographs of the objects or to allow them to have free access. In some large institutions, rights and reproductions programs have now opened the doors to free access to the images from their collection. Examples can be seen at the Metropolitan Museum of Art and the Getty. If you choose to restrict the images, make sure that you have the restriction written in your loan agreement. An example can be to restrict the image to record shots and a one-time use in the catalog.

Amending the Loan Agreement

You should guard against oral amendments to the loan agreement. It is too easy to have a misunderstanding. There should be a clause that the agreement may be amended only in writing and must be signed by both parties.

LOAN NUMBERS AND A LOAN REGISTER

Museums that borrow a lot of material often keep a loan register and assign numbers to each borrowed item. This is a good idea if you are mounting four or six large loan exhibits a year or have a large turnover in loans. Loan registers are normally kept only for loans to the museum. You already have a record of your own objects, and the loan register gives you control over all the objects in the museum that are not part of your collection. Some museums also keep a register of objects loaned from the museum, but I do not think that is necessary, unless you have an inordinate number of loans. Loan numbers were discussed in chapter 3 but are assigned only to items you borrow; your own objects have accession numbers. A loan register may look like the example in the appendix. The loan register should be checked periodically and the status of all loans cleared. At the end of the year, the register and all loans should be up to date and the status of all loans reported to the board.

I am only suggesting a loan register, as it is an excellent device to keep track of loans, if you have a number of loans during the year. I doubt that it would be necessary to have the loan register if you have fewer than five transactions a year. Whether the loan register would be helpful depends on the staff and the time you have available. Keeping all the documents on loans in a file or filing system is another way of tracking them.

If your collections management database has a module for entering loan information, this is an excellent way of keeping track of these items. This is particularly true if you have many loaned items to track.

CONSERVATION LOANS

Museums often lend or borrow things for conservation or identification. These transactions are handled pretty much the same way as any other loan. When the museum lends out an object to be conserved, the administration should have a good idea what the conservator is going to do with it. The conservator should look at the object before it is sent to him or her and then state in writing what he or she proposes to do. If this is impossible, the object is sent to the conservator for examination first. The conservator will then report back on the proposed treatment. If that is agreeable, the institution will usually sign off on a contract or treatment proposal. This description of work can also be attached to or included in the loan form. The agreement should give the conservator the flexibility to allow the conservator to make some changes to the proposed treatment if he or she runs into problems and tight enough to prevent him or her from doing more than the museum staff wishes. The time limits have to be somewhat looser on these loans, as the conservator will often run into problems, and you do not want to hurry the conservator, but there should be a finite time limit. Loans can always be extended.

If the museum is fortunate enough to have staff trained in conservation, they will sometimes do conservation work for outsiders. When that is done, the transaction becomes a business deal and not a museum function. The museum should have the protections that any business has, particularly liability coverage. One of the many ways to justify the cost of a conservation laboratory is the ability to use the excess capacity of the lab for outside work. In these instances, the museum should have strict procedures regarding what it takes in for conservation work.

TEMPORARY DEPOSITS OR "DROP-OFF" LOANS

If someone leaves an object at the museum, even without the knowledge or permission of the museum, that object is likely the museum's responsibility until it is returned. Museums also take in temporary deposits to consider for potential donation, research, and so on. For these reasons, it is best to have a policy about what is to be received at the museum. This is especially important in volunteer-run museums, where there may be a large number of people working at the reception area of the museum over the course of the year. It might be best to have a simple statement, like the following example, placed where every volunteer can see it.

If anyone brings in an object with the offer to donate, sell, or lend it to the Hero County Historical Society, the object may not be accepted or left at the museum without the permission of Mrs. Supreme Optimist, XXX–XXXX, or Mrs. Usually Negative, XXX–XXXX. If they are not available, inform the potential donor that the Society may be interested in their object, but that you may not receive it, and that the potential donor should make an appointment with the staff members listed above.

If permission is granted, then the proper form can be signed, so that both parties know their responsibilities.

In instances such as this, the museum may find it useful to have a "temporary deposit" or "temporary custody" form that allows prospective donors to temporarily leave items at the museum while awaiting action. A deposit form allows museums to keep the object for a short period of time, pending the preparation of other forms, but does not obligate them as deeply as a loan form or gift agreement might. A sample deposit form is appendix A-11.

People will often bring things to the museum for identification. It is a good practice to have a policy on this. I recommend not doing it at all. If a museum accepts an object for identification, it is a loan just as much as any other loan. It should be treated accordingly. If the museum receives no real benefit from the loan, there is a question as to whether it should be accepted at all. Some museums have a separate form for identification or conservation loans, but I do not think it is necessary.

A procedure such as the one outlined above can prevent awkward situations where you have to track down the donor to tell him or her you are not interested in the piece. It also helps prevent you from dealing with abandoned property situations.

EXISTING LONG-TERM LOANS

There is no such thing as a permanent loan; either it is a loan or it is not. Lawyers have a fascinating language. Loans can be considered a "gratuitous bailment without the right of survivorship."[4] Most attorneys will agree that the loan never becomes the museum's property, no matter how long it is kept, though that situation has been changed, as most states have added abandoned property legislation to assist museums. As I pointed out earlier, there may be a good reason to take in a long-term loan, but never kid yourself that it is yours. It is best to have such loans on a one- or two-year basis, and then neither party will forget the status of the property.

Laws on abandoned property vary widely, and there may be some way to claim legal title. As of 2013, forty-six states and the District of Columbia had this legislation on the books. It is a good idea to check your state's laws though because the terms vary widely and in some states the law only applies to state museums.[5]

Acquiring the title to the property can be tricky and is always subject to question if the owner or heirs appear. In one case, the heirs showed up more than ninety years later. The only thing that kept the items in the museum was the fact that there were twenty heirs and they could not agree on who got the objects. Even under such circumstances, the objects do not belong to the museum, nor will they ever, under the laws of that state. In other cases, where the museum follows the abandoned property laws of the state and the owner and/or heirs do not come forward, the museum may be able to claim the title.[6]

The best method of clearing up such loans is to attempt to track down the original lenders or their heirs and to try to get them to donate the objects or to claim them. That is a time-consuming and unpleasant task, but it may be necessary. When you try to clear up long-term loans, you often risk losing a valuable object, but that is better than offering free storage.

WHAT NOT TO DO AND WHEN NOT TO DO IT

There are a lot of variable with loans but one of the most important is to make sure you get everything in writing. Loans are usually made to people with whom the museum is acquainted. There is a tendency to be a bit careless on procedure when the object has no great value or the deal is between friends. If you have a loan procedure, it is a good idea to stick to it. That way, if any questions come up, you will have the details in writing.

Many things about loans that should not be done fall into the curatorial area rather than the area of registration, and so are outside the scope of this book. The person making the loan must ensure that the object will be taken care of when it is out of the museum and that the loan will not bring discredit to the museum. For that reason, I am always leery of loans for promotional purposes. You never know if you lend a carriage to an automobile dealer for promotion that you will not see it prominently displayed in the media with a caption like "Look at this stupid, creaky old carriage that we got from the historical society. Why drive this when you could drive a Total?"[7] These days, this is more likely to be a loan to a television show, where you may or may not like the way your artifact is portrayed.

It is wise to make sure that any prospective borrowers who are unknown to you are who they say they are and really represent the organization they claim to represent. We usually insist that the borrowers write to us on the organization's stationary, stating what they want to borrow and how they intend to display it.

Loans to the museum tend to be carefully made and cared for until the exhibit is over, and then the pressure is off. You may get a little careless then. That loan is your baby until the owner has it in hand and is satisfied with its condition. Do not relax the care of the piece for even a minute.

When a museum borrows or lends an object, it places its reputation on the line. A carefully thought-out loan procedure will prevent most problems. Remember, in 999 cases out of 1,000, things go well. The one time when there is a problem is the one that causes all the trouble. The loan policy of the museum should be such that it handles the 999 cases well and has all its homework done for the one problem case.

NOTES

1. Malaro, *Primer*, 273–54, has an extensive discussion of the legal aspect of loans; Phelan, *Museum Law*, 223–31, has a more limited discussion of loans. See also Sally Freitag, Cherie Summers, and Judy Cline, "Loans," in Buck and Gilmore, *MRM5*, 120–32 and passim. AAM Registrars Committee, Professional Practices Subcommittee, "Loan Survey Report," May 1990, reported some rather interesting things. One was that 21 percent of history museums did not have a loan policy. I could not find more recent statistics on the subject, but this probably has not changed much in small history museums.

2. Marie Demeroukas, Deborah Rose Van Horn, and Heather Culligan, "General Condition Reporting: An Overview," in *Basic Condition Reporting*, 1–6.

3. AAM Registrars Committee, *General Facilities Report* (Arlington, VA: The AAM Press, 2011). RC-AAM recently changed its name to the Collections Stewardship Professional Network. The work may be found through the professional network's website or through the AAM bookstore.

4. Daniel Reibel, *Registration Methods for the Small Museum*, 4th ed., 114.

5. Several professional organizations keep listings of states with abandoned property laws on their websites. These lists are updated periodically. A few of these organizations include the Society of American Archivists, the Association of Registrars and Collections Specialists, and the Registrars Committee of the American Alliance of Museums. (All three had listings accessible as of December 18, 2016.)

6. Malaro, *Primer*, 327–38, 339–42, and 343–54; Ildiko Pogany DeAngelis, "Old Loans," and Kathryn Speckart, "Old Loans: State Legislation," in Buck and Gilmore, *MRM5*, 85–90 and 91–96; Anita Manning, "Converting Loans to Gifts," *AASLH Technical Leaflet #94* (Nashville: AASLH, 1977). Phelan, *Museum Law*, 223–29, discusses the two types of gratuitous bailments depending on the "benefit" one gets from the loan.

7. Be aware that you may be creating a precedent when you lend objects to a commercial or noneducational agency that may force you to lend museum items to agencies for purposes you would rather not; Malaro, *Primer*, 291–93.

A World of Computers

Computers are now a common tool in most registration systems. However, one thing to remember is that the computer is just a machine and is only as good as the information you put into it.[1]

I am going to suggest an approach to computers that will fit the small museum. I am going to assume that the reader knows enough about computers to make intelligent choices or can acquire this knowledge. I will not be too specific in this chapter, as the technology changes so quickly that if I get too technical, the advice will be obsolete before this book is published.

A collections management program should be able to do the following things:

- Store data in a useful format
- Edit data
- Delete data
- Access the data in some useful form including making "string searches"—that is, all the records where certain words appear in any combination such as "fan back" and "Windsor"
- Sort data in various ways but particularly in what is called a "dictionary sort"—that is, in strict alphabetical and numerical order
- Edit and write reports to paper or screen

FIRST STEPS

A lot of the failures in using computers result from poor planning. You have to know what you really need before you buy anything. The first thing you should do is make a "needs assessment" of your museum. The people involved in the collection should get together and develop a list of things they would like to get from the registration system. An analysis of actual searches for information is useful. It will help you begin to understand where you go to look for information and what you look for. A step-by-step analysis of the most common processes, such as accessioning, loans, catalog searches for exhibits, updating catalogs, donor requests, inventories, and so on, is very useful. There is no particular format for this form, but these lists will show you who needs to know what, how much they need to know, in what form, and how often the information is needed. Just as important, they show you what information you do not need. See textbox 8.1 for an analysis tool for a record search.

A look at your policies and procedures is also in order. Do your current records reflect museum policy? What about your procedures? Do you still need all of the paper forms that you used to have? It is often easier to enter information directly into your database. If you are moving from a manual system to a computer, you will need to consider these processes and more.

EXAMPLE OF THE ANALYSIS OF A TYPICAL CARD CATALOG FILE SEARCH

Subject of search: "Typical tools on a cabinetmaker's workbench."

Actions:	Analysis:
Make a list of the tools needed: a bench; types of planes, braces, bits, saws, hammers, clamps, rulers, squares, etc. Sometimes this is done mentally.	Chenhall has a classification for this that would pull up these at once.
Search catalog for requisite cards. Search main entry catalog. Look through entire tool catalog. Remove cards as potential objects are found.	The ability to flag, or mark, particular records would be useful so that after the initial search we can find these records again.
List objects by name, number, and location.	The program must be able to generate a report for this purpose.
Search storage for objects.	How are we going to mark location? Should objects "live" at one spot? Shelf lists would be useful.
Return cards to file.	
Assemble objects in dummy exhibit. Select ones for use.	The flag system has to allow for the objects to be placed on exhibit or returned to their proper place in storage.
	If there is need to borrow objects for the exhibit, we need the ability to account for this.
Set up exhibit.	We need to be able to easily extract information for labels. We need to be able to easily extract donor names for labels. We need to know if there are restrictions on identifying donors. We need the ability to track objects while on exhibit.
Orient interpreters, write hand-out literature.	Need the ability to pull up information for training purposes. It would be useful to transport catalog information for labels and training guides.
Take down exhibit.	Need to track objects back to storage.

You will also have to consider who will have access to the database. This is a great opportunity to update your security procedures to include access to data. Does every staff member and volunteer need to be able to edit records? Do you implement different levels of access and editing capabilities? Should everyone be able to delete a record? These are all things you will need to think about.

Then you are ready to start making up a list of fields you want to include. A field is a discrete piece of information, such as the accession number. You can be quite generous to yourself while making up this list of fields. Put in every field that you think you may need. The list can (and will) be cut down later. Start thinking about what the field should contain. Should it be only text? Should it be only numbers? How long should the field be (often the number of characters)? These decisions only need to be general ideas at this stage, as the type of software you select will have a great deal of bearing on the number and the makeup of the fields. A reduced list of the fields, recommended by the Common Agenda Data Bases Task Force, is in chapter 4, but see the section on the number of fields below.

The most important things to remember is that if you want to get a particular piece of data out of the system (measurements, provenance, etc.), you must put that information into the system. If you are going to require new fields to capture information that is not currently in your records, you should have a plan for how you should acquire that information. You should also look at the information that is already in the system. If you never look at the information in one of the fields, do you really need it?

It is often tempting to get the complex system with all the bells and whistles. It is often better to get the simpler system with some fields that can be customized to meet your actual needs.

THE NUMBER OF FIELDS

In its day, the catalog card was a very effective data storage device. You could get only a limited amount of data on it so its small size promoted efficient use of data. In their mass, the cards were almost impossible to use effectively and stored enormous amounts of redundant data but had a brute efficiency for storing essential data.[2]

When computers first began to have a large impact on the museum field (late 1960s and 1970s) a favorite input/output device was also a card, a punch card, though some data was stored on tape. Each card held about eighty bits of data, though techniques were developed to have more on a card or more than one card in a record. Rather than put every card through the machine each time you wanted to address the computer or get all your data reels out, systems were developed to classify the terminology, an index as it were, so that you only had to put a drawer or two of cards through the machine instead of every card in the file. This may seem hopelessly slow and clumsy compared to today's technology, but it was incredibly fast by the standards then.

In the absence of adequate indices, one had lots of fields. Curators used to get together and discuss the number of fields they had and try to top each other: "You have 110 fields? Wow, I have 220." As computers got bigger and faster, the number of fields diminished.

Because computers were so slow by today's standards, the classification systems perpetuated the idea that museum registration systems had to be able to be broken down into families, even when we advanced beyond punch cards. The system adapted by the history museum field was Robert G. Chenhall's *Nomenclature.*[3]

As we have discussed above, until Chenhall there was no single classification system for the history museum field. His system gave us a way of making the English language act like a systematic language. Chenhall's system was widely adopted by the history museum field and, to a lesser extent, by the art and anthropology fields.

Though originally intended for computerized collections, the Chenhall system worked well with paper records. In fact, the naming convention, with the noun first followed by the modifier, provided a good sorting method, if not a classification system. For many museums, Chenhall proved more valuable for the naming conventions than it ever was for its classification system. His classification system was more useful in large museums with varied collections though it still has its uses in the smallest collection.

Later on there were "authority lists." These were mainly developed by the art museum world, of which Peterson's *Art and Architecture Thesaurus* is the best known and the most widely adopted in the museum field. Rather than provide a single term for each object, these lists provided almost every term, though one term usually could be designated as "preferred." These authority lists were so large, hard to administer, and relatively expensive that they were mainly adopted by large museums.

In the 1990s the PC became large enough, fast enough, and cheap enough so that any museum could afford one. Computers superseded almost all manual systems of registration. A number of museums developed their own electronic registration system with varying success. Today most museums of any size have at least some of their collection in a computerized form. We went back to lots of fields.

So, what does this have to do with anything? The computers used by the early systems were so small that a collection record had to be small and efficient. Today, the record can be almost any size, but the people remain the same. I have an ideal size for a museum collection when discussing abstracts. It is 10,000 objects. If you have fifty fields in my ideal-sized museum, then you have 500,000 blank spaces in your system that need to be filled with data. If you have 100 fields, you have the potential for a million pieces of data for your collection. Do you need that much data? Probably not. I challenge you to count the number of fields in your museum's system and then multiply it by the size of your collection. You will be surprised by the number of fields you actually have to address.

All the Fields You Will Ever Need

I think almost all museums can get along with fifteen to twenty fields if they need to. Much of the information that is being parsed out to other fields can be included in the description, and then you can let the computer do the searches. For my 10,000-object collection, there are still 150,000–200,000 potential fields to fill out. This is enough for most small museums to handle.

If you analyze a typical search for useful information in your present system, you will find that you are probably only using 10–15 percent of the data. You seldom need to know that it is painted blue or has astragal ends. What you usually look for is very simple and very specific.

This is the information asked for in most searches of a museum catalog:

- Accession number
- Type of object ("genus" and "species")
- Classification (*Nomenclature*)
- How acquired (gift, purchase, etc.)
- Source (donor, from whom purchased, etc.)
- Location
- Material
- Size
- Place of origin
- Maker
- Date (of manufacture)
- Description
- Association
- Image
- Comment
- Value
- Flag

This record of seventeen fields contains most of the information that you will ever need. With some clever manipulation, you can get these fields on one screen. A record of this length can support sophisticated questions such as the location of all silver tea sets with gadrooning made in Boston before 1810 by specific makers. However, it is also manageable for a museum with one professional staff member to do the data entry.

Accession Number

This numbering field is very important as it tied the object to the records. If you have two or more numbering systems, an extra field or fields for the other numbering systems can be useful. Using these extra number fields, you can utilize some of the old numbering systems when necessary. The computer can also show the relationship between the several numbering systems.

Title and Classification

As we have discussed, these fields are used to identify and classify the object. For reasons of clarity and ease of entry, you need a separate field for the title and the classification. If you do not have a large collection, you might be able to skip the classification field.

How Acquired

Using this field, you can separate out the donations from the purchases and other means of acquisition. If you have long-term loans and deaccessions, this field will help you identify them. The field need be only one letter long—as an example, L for "loan." Some museums call this the "status" field.

Source

The source field is a useful field that is used constantly in museums with any number of donations. In the case of purchases, this field can be where it was purchased, or, if money had been donated for the purchase, it can be used to indicate the contributor of the funds used in the purchase. In these cases, you can enter the vendor in the "Comments" field in case you need to know this information later.

Location

The best way to indicate location in a computer is to have the object "live" at one location and track it only when it is moved. This is discussed in chapter 6 on cataloging.

Material

The effectiveness of the material field depends on what the material is. When the object is made mainly of one material, such as glass, silver, tin, or wrought iron, then you will find it a useful way to find or classify certain objects. When there are many materials, such as in an automobile or a chair made of seven different woods, the field will be nearly useless for creating a class but very useful for identification. It is better to be specific in terminology when possible: "maple" instead of "wood."

Size

The size field is a lot more useful in a computer than it is in a paper catalog. If you have a separate field for width, height, depth, or diameter, you can extract the number of running feet objects slated for an exhibit will need or the cubic volume of the collection. If the size is to be used in this fashion, the dimensions have to be entered decimally. Size fields can be configured to give either inch/foot or metric measurements and can convert one automatically to the other.

Place of Origin

Where the object originated is of great importance as that often influences the style, material, method of construction, or even how the object was used. It is better to be specific ("Boston" rather than "New England") when possible. In some collections, the place of use will be important, and you may need a separate field for that as well.

Maker

The "Maker" field is actually the "Creator" field. You should list the artist, engraver, craftsman, manufacturer, and printer as well as publisher and any other person or entity that had a hand in the creation of the object. If the maker is a school or group (Shakers, U.S. Navy, etc.), that should be indicated here.

Date of Manufacture

The date of manufacture is very important, but this is where you have to insist on rigid standards. The computer cannot tell the difference between "ca. 1840," "c. 1840," and "1835–1845." You have to pick one method. I do not like the use of around (ca.) in a computer database, as it is vague and difficult to access or sort. I prefer to use a range of dates, such as "1770–1800" for either "later 18th century" or "ca. 1784." In buying or implementing software, see how well the program handles a range of dates. You may need two fields for a beginning and an ending date.

Description

The description will be a very useful thing if you can enter all that data. If you have a description field, make sure that your program will search the description field for the data you need. You need to be able to perform "string searches" that allow you to search for relationships such as all the records that contain the words "bow back" and "Windsor." In that fashion, you can find all of the Windsor chairs with bow backs without having a style field. Instead of a separate field for information such as user or color, include them in the description. This cuts down on the number of fields and gives you a great deal of flexibility in searches. See chapter 6 on cataloging.

Association

The computer makes it easier to search for an association of an object with a person, place, or event than a card catalog. It is important that your program can make "string searches" for useful data, such as the relationship of George Washington with the Whiskey Rebellion. When entering this information into the computer, you will have to have strict rules on how this information is to be entered if you expect to make any kind of search of this field. This is a time-consuming field to create, but once it is done, you will use it often.

Image

If you use a digital image as part of the registration program, then you need an image field. If you have it as a separate image file, then you have to indicate in the registration program that you have a file and where it is located.

Comment

A "comment" field is also useful for all that information that is not included in other fields.

Value

Some museums place a value on each object in the collection. You can manipulate this value. You can get a total value for the collection or a portion of it, you could upgrade the value if prices rise, or you can get a value for just a part of the collection. You can use it to assess risk for insurance purposes. For example, you can find out what your risk is in certain areas ("the total value of the objects stored in room 101"). It could give you a total on a certain class of objects, such as all the silver. Some programs will even round off these values when you raise them. This field can be helpful if you need to reassess your insurance needs or find out how much a piece should be insured for before it goes out on loan. As I said before, some museums do not place a value on the collection. If you do not, you can eliminate this field.

Flag

A flag field is useful. You can "flag" certain groups of objects that are otherwise unrelated. For instance, you can "flag" a group of unrelated objects that are to be loaned to another museum and call up their records anytime by their flag. That saves calling up each record individually. Most flag fields are either a check box or a two-character field. The two-character field has its advantages because you can create a range of flags from a–zz or 00–99.

Condition

I have not included a condition field in the ones above, but it would be useful to have a few fields set aside for this purpose. First would be a field for a ranking method. A simplified ranking method can help prioritize conservation needs. Many museums use the terms "excellent," "good," "fair," and "poor." An alternative method is to use a numbering system such as the following:

"1"   indicates the condition "Urgent." The object needs immediate care.

"2"   indicates the condition "Serious But Not Urgent." The safety of the object is in jeopardy and its condition will become urgent if not conserved.

"3"   indicates the condition "Requires Treatment." If stored properly, the treatment may be delayed.

"4"   indicates the condition "Exhibitable." Should be exhibitable if handled carefully.

"5"   indicates the condition "Good." The object is exhibitable and requires maintenance only to stay in the present condition.

Other condition fields you may require would be a "description of condition" field, an "examiner" field, and a "condition date" field. The "description of condition" field allows you to take notes so that you can see if the condition gets worse over time. The "examiner" field lets you know who the last person to look at the condition was, and the "date" field lets you know when it was last examined.

SOFTWARE

Now that you have decided what fields you need and what types of searches you will need your system to perform, you are in a better position to evaluate the proposals of software vendors.

When you want to file something with paper records you buy a filing cabinet and folders. It is the same idea with a database system. You need to look at the systems and evaluate what you need to buy. In some cases, you may need other compatible software, and some programs will work on some computers while they are not set up to work on others (Apple vs. a PC). You will also want to find something that you and your staff can easily use. The operation of computers is not readily apparent to everyone, and software choices can be bewildering in their number and complexity.

If you are starting from scratch, you should select the software before you select the hardware. The kind of software we will probably be looking at is so-called application software. An application program is the one you use to perform certain structured tasks on the computer such as word processing, spreadsheets, desktop publishing, and, of course, data management.

The kind of application software that you will probably use for registration is some form of a data management program. These programs have the ability to create, edit, index, and sort data, and then display the results on the screen or paper. They usually have a report-building utility built in and will be able to work with a word-processing program to create documents from the data in your collection. The system should also have the ability to import data from or export data to other programs or applications. Most commercial collections management systems have these abilities. If you are creating your own database with a commercial database system, you will need to make sure that it has these abilities too.

The best-known type of data management program is a "relational database" program. This kind of program relates each piece of data in your database through a series of related fields and tables. Not all data management systems are relational, but that does not mean that the ones that are not relational are not useful. Many users will not be able to tell the difference between a relational database and one that is not relational.

Many consultants or companies take another company's software and adapt it to specific situations. They are often called third-party vendors, or resellers, or value-added dealers (VAD) or value-added retailers (VAR). Almost all of your museum-specific programs, such as collections management systems, will come from third-party vendors of one kind or another. There are two choices for you:

- An off-the-shelf collections management program that has been developed as a product specific to the museum field
- A proprietary program written specifically for you by a third party

The advantage of the off-the-shelf program is that you do not have to reinvent the wheel. Many of these programs are advertised in museum journals and demonstrated at professional meetings. Most museum people find these products to be adequate, and many find that the simpler the program, the better. The advantage of the proprietary program is that it can be tailored to your specific needs, but they can also be expensive and often do not have a team that can answer questions when you have a problem.

In dealing with vendors, keep this in mind: You are not buying a program; you are buying a registration system! The vendor will be talking about the "program," and you will be talking about the "system." Make sure you are both talking about the same thing.

There are a bewildering number of possibilities, and it is difficult enough for an expert to pick the right one, let alone a novice. You will be better able to make a choice if you look at these considerations:

- What do you want the program to do? Is it to be a complete registration system performing all of the functions of your old manual registration system? Or will it be an electronic catalog? If you have made your needs assessment, you will be better able to assess this choice.
- Does the vendor have a client list? He or she should. Get the names of nearby museums that are similar in scope and size to yours that use the software. Contact those museums and *go look* at the system in operation. There is nothing like an opinion from a user, or several users, to find out how the program really works. If the vendor has never done a museum program, he or she should be able to supply a client list with needs similar to yours.
- Almost all the third-party systems have several screens. A screen is a specific view of a number of fields in your database. Can you easily get to the screen you want, or do you have to flip from screen to screen every time you want to look at something? Instead of having the vendor demonstrate for you, sit down at the machine and try it

yourself! To be useful, these screens require a lot of data entry. Do you need all this information? Can you enter all of it and keep it updated?

- The manuals or websites that come with the various programs are important. Can you actually find the help you need in these publications? Can you read and understand it? Does it provide specific information that will help you solve your problem, or is it just helpful hints?

- Your data is worthless unless it can be read by a program. So, the ability of more than one company's program to read your data is a survival characteristic. When you look at the program that your system is based upon, you assess the "portability" of the data that is generated by this program—that is, the ability to transfer the data to other programs and other computers. The primary reason for this is that programs do not last forever, vendors go out of business, hardware changes, and better programs come along. The other reason is that you may want to use the data in other programs to create useful documents or perform some other function. If you can't make this assessment, then try to get advice from an expert. You have to assume that the most widely vended application software programs are portable, but this is not always true. If in doubt, make the vendor show you that it is!

- You need copies of the software containing the various programs that actually operate the registration system. In the past, this software would have come on disks, but now it is often a download. Without the software, you cannot make changes to your program and perhaps are not able to transport it. Normally, the vendor gives you a package consisting of the program (or access to it), program manuals, and anything else that is needed to make it work. But some vendors do not use this method, and you must make sure that you have the "source" programs, or the basic applications, that will interact with your computer, or with others. Otherwise, you may not be able to alter, upgrade, or transport your program without the vendor—who may or may not be available, or with whom you may not wish to do business.

- Can the vendor adapt the package specifically for your museum or must you take it as sold? If the vendor can adapt it, is there a fee to do this? If it is as sold, is this the program that you want?

- Is the program written for your type of museum? Many programs are written for other types of museums and then adapted to history museums. A test of usefulness is whether they have a field for classification. If you have done your needs assessment well, then you will be able to make a judgment about the usefulness of the program.

- Does the vendor give on-site training? If so, how much training? Is there a fee for this?

- Does the vendor support the program either over the telephone or online? Is there a charge for this? Check with people on the vendor's client list to see how well they perform this service.

- In the case of proprietary programs, the program should be a "work for hire." That is, the copyright is the museum's property. You should not be restricted in how you can adapt or use the program or which vendor you can use to update it. The original vendor may not be around when needed. Moreover, you do not want to pay a vendor the start-up costs to develop a program that he or she will market widely. However, the vendor may not want to create a program for you that you will sell or give away far and wide with no benefit to the vendor. You will have to reach an agreement with the vendor on this. I would warn you away from any deal where only the original vendor may update the program.

DO IT YOURSELF

You have another choice. If you are familiar with computers, you may be able to adapt an application yourself. You become your own third-party vendor. This may prove to be an excellent way for a small museum that can define its goals and keep things simple. This is also a procedure that the museum has to approach very cautiously. I know of two cases when someone worked on one of these adaptations for a long period of time—in both cases, several years—and never produced a useful program.[4]

Any program produced should be in some readily available application program; it should be updateable; and it should be exportable to other programs.

The museum should have an agreement with the staff member doing this on the goals of the program, a time-table, and a measurement of success. Documentation (a user manual) should be part of the package. I would not get into this unless:

- The staff member is already familiar with programming or adapting applications. It is not a good idea for someone to learn to program on your time and make all of their mistakes in your museum.
- There is some mutually agreed-upon measure of the success of the program. A simple measurement would be that the program would answer the needs discovered in your needs assessment, be useable to any staff member, be able to do sophisticated searches (find all the bow back Windsor chairs made in Hero County before 1800), be able to produce a certain number and type of reports, have a user manual, and have a data dictionary.
- The program can be completed in a specific time frame—usually no longer than a third-party vendor would take to develop the same program.

I adapted an application program at the Old Barracks Museum.[5] I spent three months working with the old records and collection in developing an idea of our needs before I even bought an application program. This advance work would have been needed for any type of program selected. I had the museum's program created and up and running in about four hours, but then I had designed the program to use only one screen. I updated it a little after that, as I found things had been forgotten or never used. I wrote a thirty-page user manual with data standards for the system. I must say that it would have been a lot cheaper to buy one of the museum-specific programs, but the museum did not have the funds; however, they did have my salary. Of course, the Old Barracks had a program that fitted their specific needs. I understand it has since been transported to another application program and a different computer, so it has passed that test as well.

SOMETHING TO THINK ABOUT

A third-party system will have been tried and tested for applicability in many museums and should be up and running within a few minutes of being installed. However, it will be designed to fit the needs of a wide range of museums. The proprietary program may suit your needs best, match unusual hardware requirements, and will include things that no other program has, but it will take a lot more money, time, and work. The small museum may find that it can keep costs down and usefulness up by creating its own program.

HARDWARE

I have not discussed hardware very much. Many museums will not have a choice in the hardware (it was donated, the city gave every employee the same type of computer, etc.), but if you do save it until after the software selection, you will find that the choice of hardware is relatively simple. You probably cannot have too fast a machine, too much storage (hard drive space), or too much RAM memory, but the practical consideration of cost will govern that to some extent. It is a good idea to buy at least twice as much storage space as you will ever need, if not more. Three or four times would not be too much even if this storage is on an external hard drive or in a cloud storage.

In dealing with personal computers, I would recommend only buying hardware that has a configuration that has a wide popular acceptance—that is, it is made by well-known manufacturers and has well-understood industry-wide standards. When you buy a machine with a configuration that only one manufacturer makes, then you are at their mercy, and software choices are more limited.

I am equally reluctant to buy a software program that will run on only one particular manufacturer's computer. This is so-called hardware-specific software. The data should be transportable, though you may have more limited choices.

FREE COMPUTERS

Many times small museums are offered a free machine by someone who is upgrading his or her own computer. These are usually old but functional devices sitting around in someone's home or business. One thing to remember is that computer software and hardware become obsolete very quickly. The shelf life of a software program is three years or less, and hardware updates come out so rapidly that a new computer is usually obsolete in a year. A gifted computer may be slow and have limited capacity by current standards. The problem with these gifts is that turning them away may be difficult. As diplomatically as possible, one should try to get a new computer of sufficient size and speed dedicated to collection uses. An argument you might be able to use is that the "free" computer may cost more to update and maintain than a new one.

NETWORKS

If there are a number of computers in the museum, it may pay to set up a local area network (LAN). If the museum has facilities scattered over a region, or is statewide or national, then you may need a wide area network (WAN). These are two different kinds of networks and may require different hardware and software. These networks can be difficult to set up if you have never done it before, and it may require bringing in an expert to set it up for you. There may be a savings to offset the cost of the networks, as you will have increased ability to communicate, see higher efficiency, may not need as sophisticated a terminal for everyone, and can share software, printers, faxes, and scanners.

Enforcing network-wide discipline requires some sophisticated management techniques. If you install a network on more than two or three machines, you had better be prepared to spend some time on administering the network. Both types of network require extensive security measures, particularly the WAN.

THE CLOUD

Another option that is being utilized by some museums is a cloud storage or cloud network. Cloud computing is where the storage or networking is done on the Internet. There are many different cloud options, as major companies like Google, Amazon, Microsoft, IBM, and others have begun to offer their own cloud computing options (think Google Drive, Dropbox, etc.). There are too many of these options out there right now, but some museums are using cloud computing to store or share data.

Another thing to be aware of is that many of the proprietary systems are now looking at the cloud to host their programs. Of course, this is just the next stage in the evolution of the programs, and this may be obsolete in a few years as well.

DATA ENTRY AND TESTING

A program is useless until the data is entered into the database. Data entry is a real chore and the place where many computer projects go wrong. The data in most paper records will not translate easily to a computer record. Until the data conforms to specific standards, it will not be very useful. There are several ways to handle the initial capture of information in your file.

- You can develop a "data capture sheet" that has a place for every field in the computer program. This is a version of the worksheet discussed earlier; you should design one of these to fit your own needs. You can update the data as you enter it on the form. Then inexperienced data-entry persons can enter the information into the computer. This may be the best method, but it will take a lot longer than other methods before you have entered enough data to be useful—an awful lot longer. (See an example of the data capture sheet in figure 8.1.) This is the last paper document you generate in the accessioning process. If you do not print out your worksheet, you should archive this form.

- You can update the information as you enter it from the original records. This will require trained people to do the data entry, though they do not necessarily have to be the professional staff. They can be volunteers. I used this system at the Old Barracks Museum and found that it was efficient and produced useable data almost instantly.

- Or you can enter the data as it is and update it afterward. Untrained people can do the data entry, but a trained person is going to have to go through each record and correct it. This is a method that a small museum might consider, as you get useable data almost from the start. There are "optical character readers" (OCRs) that may be able to read your old data into your new files. If you have a large collection file, an OCR may be worth exploring.

In any case, the professional staff is going to have to check each record. You can get the computer to do some of the updating for you, or at least find some of the errors (such as all the objects without measurements).

To avoid data-entry fatigue early in the process, I would suggest a simple procedure. I would suggest a very simple record with only three fields: the number and name of the object, and its location. Any unskilled data-entry person can do this and you will end up with a complete file of your collection. Then you can go back and round off each record.

THE HERO COUNTY HISTORICAL SOCIETY
DATA CAPTURE SHEET

Accession Number:
Old Number:
Title of Object:
Classification:
Source:
Pair or set:
Material:
Size:
Place of origin:
Maker:
Association:
Value:
Date of manufacture:
Conservation Priority:
Description:

Image no.

Comments:

FIGURE 8.1.
Data Capture Sheet

Data Dictionary

You will need a "data dictionary." This is a document that sets standards for data. You might be able to tell that "stockings, pair," "stockings, pr.," "pair of stockings," and "stockings (a-b)" all mean the same thing, but a computer cannot without very complicated instructions. For most applications, you will have to pick one way or another to enter data, and you must establish similar standards for each data field. However, you can configure fields to accept only certain types of data, or only accept certain words, or to make the field conform to a standard, or automatically adapt the data to your specifications. This ability mitigates, to a limited extent, the need for rigid standards.

Testing Your Data

When you start up a program it is a good idea to enter a few records and test the system. Enter about one hundred records and try it out. You will discover many of the problems of data entry and idiosyncrasies of the program. Later, when you have a thousand or so records, you ought to do this again. A file of the latter size will also give you an idea of how much space the whole file is going to take up on your disk and give you an accurate estimate of the time required to enter all the museum records.

Many museums find that volunteers can enter data if they have some training. Entering data is the most expensive part of the project, and using volunteers can save you a lot of money. Once the volunteers are trained, they are a pool of people who are familiar with your system and can do all sorts of jobs for you.

HOW MANY OBJECTS DO YOU HAVE?

An interesting question comes up when you begin to enter data into a computer: How many objects does the museum have? For things such as a pair of andirons, a pair of stockings, a cup and saucer, a fireplace set, or a chess set, is there one record or several? In a paper catalog, they are often listed as one object, or at least one card. There is quite a bit of discussion in the museum field with little resolution. How you treat this depends on the kinds of results you need from the catalog. If you are just looking for a simple catalog system, then perhaps treating objects en suite with others as a single object will work. Because the computer itself is not able to make judgments on how to look at this kind of quandary, you have to make a decision on how you are going to treat the items.

One option is to treat each unit of a set as a single record (except pairs of shoes, stockings, and gloves). It gives you a better idea of the size of the collection, you can track each object better, you can make more sophisticated searches, and you can predict the cubic volume of the collection better. That means when you have a chess set, you do not have one object but thirty-four: the thirty-two chess pieces, the board, and the box the set comes in. If you make an individual record for each object in a pair or set, you may want to add a field to indicate that this object is a part of a pair or a set. I have a field for pairs and sets that lists the accession number of the first object in the suite.

The other option is to create a record for the set. If you do this, it is important to include a field for object count so that future staff knows if all the pieces or parts are there. Take the same chess set we just discussed; if you do not include the item count, future staff members may not know that there were thirty-three items when it came into the collection instead of the thirty-four described above. This may cause confusion and a search for a missing piece if the object count is not recorded somewhere. In scenarios where this method is used, I have seen staff answer the question of "how many objects do you have?" by saying that they have X number of records in the database comprising XX number of objects.

ONLINE DATABASES

Another thing to consider with a system is whether you will eventually need to publish your catalog online. Many collections management programs now have some sort of web publishing capability, whether it is hosted on your site or on theirs. Not all museums want to have an online catalog, but if this is of interest to your institution, you will also need to examine these capabilities as part of your assessment of the program.

One thing to look at is how much of your data will you want to publish. Are you publishing your entire catalog or only part of it? Are you publishing every field or only a selection of fields? These questions are just a few of the considerations you will need to look at when deciding if the software will work for you.

This is also something to consider when you start looking at the costs because there may be additional fees such as hosting fees, software costs, and so forth. You will need to look at the capabilities and costs of these applications and decide if you really want to publish your catalog online.

COST

Suppose you have just re-cataloged your museum's collection and face retyping two cards on each object in your 10,000-object museum. If it only costs you a dollar in supplies and labor to type a card, and you have two cards on each object, then you have $20,000 in catalog cards alone, plus the cost of ten to fifteen drawers of space needed to store them. Depending on the nature of the data, you can purchase a good-sized computer, an inexpensive collections management system, and enter your data for about that much money.

When you average the costs of the computer, and the usefulness of the data, a computer system does not cost anywhere near as much as manually creating, maintaining, and updating a card file. This is something you should consider when making a choice between manual or computer records, and when you update your files.

People tend to think of the hardware as the most expensive thing in the registration system, but the most expensive thing is the data. It costs a lot to create and maintain it. As an example, at the Old Barracks Museum, we had less than $2,000 worth of equipment and software but about $15,000–$20,000 worth of data.

UPDATES

It is a lot more complicated to keep the computer file up to date than the old paper records. You will find yourself spending a lot of time updating the records. One of the advantages of the computer is that an active updating process will make the system much more useful as time goes on.

While a good paper system is good for decades, the useful life of your hardware and software is about five years, if that. Think carefully about making a long-term commitment to any hardware or software configuration. You will easily have at least three computer programs that will need to be constantly updated: the adaptation of the application program you are using, the application program itself, and the computer's system program(s). The hardware itself becomes obsolete with amazing rapidity. The museum should budget at least 15 or 20 percent of the total cost of the system each year over the life of the system just for updates. Occasionally you will need more.

SECURITY

Although the security of the records of any system is important, the security of computer files is a serious concern. It is not difficult for a well-meaning person to completely destroy your database in a few minutes, and there are people out there who are not well-meaning. For this reason, full access to the database should be limited to the people who can be trusted not to compromise your data. Most data managers allow various levels of access to the files through a password system. It is an excellent idea to use passwords and security levels. There are various methods of checking updated files before they are inserted into the database. You can even make it so one person must authorize the changes.

When your computer is on a network, or can be accessed over the Internet, then you have some other security concerns. There is probably not a security system in the world that cannot be bypassed by a determined person, but you can keep most people out with "firewall" programs. You can also use encryption to protect your data. Depending on how much access you are going to allow to your records via networks and outside access, I would suggest setting up some sort of block that will restrict outside access to only those records, and those fields, that are public.

You should also have an up-to-date virus protection program installed. Viruses are programs that ride into your system on the backs of other programs or data and can completely corrupt your system. The virus protection programs can help detect and/or block these viruses.

The programs that operate your registration system are very important. The software should be "archived," that is stored in a secure space with your backups. In the past, this would have meant physical disks stored in an area that is safe from pilferage, had an ideal climate, was fireproof, and was free of electromagnetic interference. If you still store your backups on disks, you will need a place that meets these requirements. However, more and more often digital backups are stored on remote servers or cloud networks and the installation software may be a download instead of a physical disk. It is still important to save these downloads with the backup of your data, but you may not need to find a space for a physical disk.

BACKUPS

You never faced losing your whole registration system in a fraction of a second until you moved it to a computer. Sure, there was a risk of fire or water damage, but the entire system would not be wiped out in a single instant. There is no excuse for losing your data. You need to back up your files regularly. Some say that two to three times a day is not too often. It is definitely a good idea to make a correct and complete copy at the end of each day, and you should keep several days' worth of backups in reserve. In case of discovering badly corrupted data, you can then go back before the problem started and rescue your files.

In the past, you would make at least three backups at the end of the day. One would be kept in a fireproof place in the museum, such as a safe, and one would be stored off-site. However, you can buy programs that will back up your files or provide off-site storage, and many institutions now store their backups on a remote server on their network or store them in cloud storage on the Internet.

It is still a good idea to make paper backups periodically. How often is a difficult question and is often governed by the size of your collection and needs. It may take four to six hours to print 2,500 records. A printing of 10,000 records may take an entire day and be a stack of paper several feet high. You may not want to do this very often. There are computer service houses that will do this for you at a relatively modest cost if they have compatible software. Mind you, you will still need to file or store these paper records, which will also take time. Electronic backups can substitute for paper, but keep in mind that electronic records do not last without some updating on your part.

Remember something about paper records! They tend to last. Computer programs deteriorate over time and need constant care. Your application program may get so old it is useless. Without a proper application program, you cannot read your files. Printed on archival-quality paper, a computer record will survive for a very long time. In fire-resistant cabinets, paper will survive almost any fire and wetting, something a computer cannot.

Since a computer file is in a constant state of update you will want to keep a picture of your collection at a certain period of time. It is a good idea to archive a backup every so often. Once a year is usually enough, but also just before you make a major update, and other needs may require other solutions.

A COMPUTER HAS OTHER USES THAN REGISTRATION

To a small museum, the computer offers many other advantages in addition to its usefulness in the registration system. Even a very small computer can give you a sophisticated word-processing program (often with the ability to set type for newsletters, publications, and labels), and ability to handle membership lists, an ability to schedule tours and events, a method of forecasting budgets, an accounting system, a data file for such tasks as fund-raising and address lists, and many other uses. The small museum may need these things long before it needs to place its registration system in some electronic form.

CONCLUSION

The computer can perform some very sophisticated tasks for you very quickly and efficiently, but knowledge of the computer, software, application, and practices needs constant updating to be effective. If you learned to type when I did (the 1940s), you learned a skill that will last your lifetime. A computer skill lasts about five years at the most without updating. You have to be constantly updating your skills, hardware, and software. A museum has to take a very long view with a computer.

Regardless of whether you use a computer, you are still going to have to follow a set of practices similar to the ones outlined in this book. A computer offers a solution to many of the complications of a registration system and most museums already use them. Just remember, the computer is a tool, just like any other tool, and do not get carried away by the technology.

NOTES

1. I am going to use the term "computer" for any device that uses and manipulates data in an electronic form (including, but not limited to, laptops, desktops, tablets, and similar devices). Buck and Gilmore's *Museum Registration Methods*, 5th ed., has a considerable amount of information about computers in registration systems throughout the text. See particularly Suzanne Quigley and Perian Sully, "Records Management: Computerized Systems," in Buck and Gilmore, *Museum Registration Methods*, 5th ed., 161–83.

2. Daniel B. Reibel, "Classification Systems and the Size of the Registration Systems," *ALHFAM Proceedings* 27 (2005), 160–61. Delivered as an address before the ALHFAM annual meeting in 2005.

3. See Blackaby, *Nomenclature*; Lanzi et al., *Introduction to Vocabularies*.

4. For a good example, see Paul E. Rivard and Steven Miller, "Cataloging Collections—Erratic Starts and Eventual Success: A Case Study," in Fahy, *Collections Management*, 211–14.

5. The Old Barracks Museum is an eighteenth-century barracks in Trenton, New Jersey, administered by the Old Barracks Association.

Conclusion

The Final Word

All of this may seem overwhelming, but if you tackle each task as it comes up, you will find that the job goes smoothly enough. It takes real commitment to register the whole collection, but once it is done, the maintenance of the system is fairly simple. If you plan carefully, commit enough time and resources to the task, and stick to it until done, the rewards will be well worth the effort.

Appendix A

Forms

Forms are necessary, as they make sure that:

- All the information is captured in an order useful to the museum.
- Museum policy is carried out.
- There is an accounting trail so that all parties can account for their actions.

The trick is to have as few forms as possible.

With the computer being so ubiquitous, the nature of forms has changed. If the registration system is computerized, the need for many forms disappears, and the ones used can be generated by computer. In many cases, even such sacred things as ledgers and registers are kept in electronic form. Many of the forms now exist only as a particular screen in the registration program. Even in a manual system, the forms are usually generated by a computer.

Many of the examples of how forms are used appear in the text. The forms in this appendix are listed roughly in the order that they appear in the book. They are numbered sequentially from A-1 (for form 1 in appendix A) to A-14. This citation is used when the forms are referred to in the text.

For more on forms, see the following books: Buck and Gilmore, *Museum Registration Methods*, 5th ed.; Malaro, *Primer*, for several succinct forms; and, to please lawyers, Phelan, *Museum Law*, for many detailed forms. There is a large assemblage of forms in John M. A. Thompson et al., eds., *Manual of Curatorship*, especially Sheila M. Stone's "Documenting Collections," 127–35, and many form-following British practice, and also Light, 1986. It is out of print, but Kenneth D. Perry, *The Museums Form Book*, 3rd ed. (Austin: Texas Association of Museums and Mountain-Plains Museums Association, 2000), has many forms actually used by museums.

LIST OF FORMS FOUND IN APPENDIX A

A-1. Certificate of Gift Form
A-2. Printed Acknowledgment of Gift
A-3. Donation Assessment Form
A-4. Worksheet
A-5. Accessions Register
A-6. Example of Typed Accession Ledger Page
A-7. Catalog Cards
A-8. Inventory Form
A-9. Loan Form for Loans from the Museum

A-10.   Loan Form for Loans to the Museum
A-11.   Deposit Loan Forms
A-12.   Condition Report
A-13.   Loan Register
A-14.   Deaccession Forms

LIST OF FORMS FOUND IN TEXT

A-1 CERTIFICATE OF GIFT FORM

The format of the certificate, or deed, of gift form needs to agree with the laws of your state so it needs to be looked at by a lawyer. The form should contain these provisions:

1. The donor owns the object(s) and has the right to dispose of it.
2. The donor is freely giving them to the museum.
3. The donor is surrendering all rights to the objects, including copyright and trademark (if he or she owns them).
4. The donor understands that the museum:
   a. Will display the object at its discretion
   b. May not keep collections together
   c. Reserves the right to dispose of (deaccession) the object at its own discretion
5. There is a place for a signature from a responsible party from the museum.
6. There is a place for a signature from the donor(s).
7. There is a place for witnesses' signatures, if required in your state.
8. The date the form was signed.

(If the copyright or trademark is not passed to the museum, or is restricted in any way, this should be noted.)

It should be clear that the gift is to the museum. The use of this form implies that you are taking the object into your collection. It is the first step in accessioning the object(s). You should use another kind of form if you are taking the object in for purposes other than inclusion in your collection.

One should consult Malaro, *Primer*, 235–36, and Phelan, *Museum Law*, 219–22, before developing any gift agreement form. This form, and loan documents, are things best approved by the museum's attorney.

DEED OF GIFT

Hero County Historical Society

Name: _____		Date: _____	
Address: _____			
City: _____	State: _____	Zip: _____	
Phone H/W:_____	Fax: _____		

I/we convey to the Hero County Historical Society the item(s) described below as an unrestricted gift, unless otherwise noted, and transfer to the Hero County Historical Society legal title, copyright, and literary property rights to the item(s) insofar as I/we hold them.

Description of Gift:

By my signature below I accept the foregoing conditions and acknowledge reading any attached information.

This gift is given in memory of: _____

Dated:_____   _____
                                   Donor/agent

                                   _____
                                   Donor/agent

Date received:_____   Received by: _____

    THE GIFT DESCRIBED ABOVE IS ACCEPTED FOR THE HERO COUNTY HISTORICAL
                              SOCIETY

By:_____   _____   _____
          name   title   date

Accession# 2016.115

A-2 PRINTED ACKNOWLEDGMENT OF GIFT

This form should be printed on high-quality card-stock or letterhead with a matching envelope. A thank-you letter is even better. There is an example of a letter in chapter 2 on acquisitions. Some museums use both a letter and an acknowledgment form.

The Board of Trustees
of the
Hero County Historical Society
gratefully acknowledge
your gift to the collection of the Museum.

[a short list of the items in the donation might go here]

Sincerely,
[signed]
President

A-3 DONATION ASSESSMENT FORM

This form, known as the donation assessment form (or the justification for accession form), is handy because it gives collections committees some real criteria for accepting or rejecting accessions. It makes staff justify why they want to add the object to the collection. Later on, it will serve as an answer to why the museum thought the object important enough to accession, should the question ever come up. These are questions that should be answered on the form. These criteria were developed by Bruce Bazalon in the 1980s, then registrar of the Pennsylvania Historical and Museum Commission.

- Does the object have a provenance, coherent story, or identification linking it to the museum's purpose?
- Does the object duplicate another object in the museum's collection?
- What is the condition of the object?
- Does it, or will it, need conservation?
- What will this cost?
- Can the museum take care of the object?
- If the museum does not accept it, what will happen to it?
  - If it is sold on the open market, will its history be lost?
  - Will it be destroyed?
- If the museum is buying the object, does its value reflect market cost?

Hero County Historical Society
Donation Assessment

TC #:

Donor Name:
Address:
Phone Number:
Email:

Items(s) for Consideration:

Provenance:

Does it duplicate another item in the collection?

Does it or will it need conservation (if yes, include estimated cost)?

Can the museum properly care for the item(s)?

If the museum does not accept it, what will happen to it?

If this is a purchase, does the cost meet current market values?

Recommendation:

Staff member: Date:

A-4 WORKSHEET

If neatly printed on good paper, this form will do as an accession sheet.

THE HERO COUNTY HISTORICAL SOCIETY
WORKSHEET

Name of Object: Accession Number:
Old Number (if there is one):
Classification (if using *Nomenclature*):
Source: Address:
Method of Acquisition: Date:
Special Terms of Acquisition:
Value:
Location:
Physical Condition:
Description:

Part of a Pair or Set?   Material:
Place of Manufacture:
Maker/Artist/Designer/Manufacturer/Distributor: (This can be combined with the User field)

User(s):   Date:
Place of Use:
Association with Person, Place, Event, or Social, Ethnic, etc., Group:

Markings/Inscriptions:

Measurements:
Provenance:

Compiler: Date:
Comments:

The fields in this worksheet are an adaptation of fields suggested by the Common Agenda Data Bases Task Force (1989). If you are using a computer database, some of these fields can be included in the description. The fields should be arranged in the order they are to be entered or typed on the card or in the computer.

It goes without saying that if you do not intend to track the information in a field, then do not include it on your form or capture it in your computer database. There are twenty-five fields on this form, providing a potential of 250,000 entries for a museum with 10,000 objects. Make sure you can handle that much data before you incorporate every field on this form.

A-5 ACCESSIONS REGISTER

This register is for a manual system. It is used *before* the object is accessioned. Its main purpose is to keep track of numbers. It gives you a quick view of the whole collection. The example is from a three-number system. If the single-number or two-number systems are used, you will need to list every object.

Computer systems will be able to generate this ledger, if needed, *after* the objects are accessioned. An example of a computer-generated register is in the text.

Accession No.	Objects	Source	Date
2008.1	Set of china, ca. 1770–1800, 42 pcs.	Mary Jones	2/13/2008
2008.2	Plow plane, ca. 1880	William Carpenter	3/2/2008
2008.3	Tuba	Johannes S. Bach	3/21/2008
2008.4	Chess set	John Smith	4/1/2008

A log would be very similar to this but kept in a stenographer's notebook.

A-6 EXAMPLE OF TYPED ACCESSION LEDGER PAGE

■

February 19, 2008

Gift of: Mr. & Mrs. Loyal Descendent
(in the name of Noble Ancestor)
123 Beesom Street
Hero, Franklin 15555

2008.11.1   <u>Machine, broom making:</u> Consists of a rotating clamp held by a ratchet; clamp is hollow to hold broom handles; in back is device to hold wire, consisting of crank-turned square bar on which slides a wooden spool; whole meant to fit on bench; base vaguely L-shaped; whole painted black; 37½ × 27¼ × 10½ overall.

2008.11.2   <u>Clamp, broom:</u> Consists of two iron jaws worked by a lever; jaws can be raised and lowered by a ratchet and crank mechanism on left; one guide (right rear) broken; whole stands of two pieces of wood to working height; molded on lip of jaws is "Pat'd Sep. 10, 1876"; painted black; 43¾ × 14 × 30 (less handle) overall; 34" to top of handle with jaws closed.

2008.11.3   <u>Cutter, broom:</u> Consists of a tapered wooden trough; at small end is cutter of cast iron which pivots on one end and is worked by handle; a series of holes is drilled in cutter making legend, "W & D York Pa."; meant to sit on legs (missing); painted black; 44¼ × 28½ × 12½ overall with handle down.

Note: The above items belonged to Mr. Descendant's great-uncle, William Jones (early twentieth century), broom maker, who built the house at 123 Beeson Street in 1920.

■

This form can be generated from a computer database, if needed.

A-7 CATALOG CARDS

Examples of catalog cards are illustrated in chapter 6. Keep in mind that catalog cards are not the complete accession record but just the information you immediately need. If necessary, the card should lead you to the proper record.

At a minimum, the catalog card should have the name of the object and the accession number. The examples give you about the maximum and minimum information needed on a catalog card.

Notice that in the example the name of the museum appears on the bottom of the card. The information you want is at the top. The name on the card just identifies the origin of the card. It can be at any place on the card, but we recommend that you put it at the bottom so that the needed information is first.

Example of a main entry card:

Object: Plate, Dinner   **Acc. No.:** 1952.2.1
Classification: 04 Food Service
Source: Ivy Propan
Location: 101
Material: Ceramic   **Size:** 11.375 dia. × 0.875
Maker: Clews   **Place Made:** England
Date: ca. 1830   **Association:** Lafayette

Description:
Flat bowl with curving sides; marley curves up; lip faintly scalloped; foot ring; underglaze blue transfer of lading of Lafayette over white ground; on bottom is stamp between two circles, "Clews Warranted safe [illegible]"; and, in underglaze blue, "The Landing of Lafayette at Castle Garden New York 16th August 1824."

HERO COUNTY HISTORICAL MUSEUM

A-8 INVENTORY FORM

You use something like this when you are not using the records or there are no records. If you use this form with good records, you will have to do a lot of flipping through records, as the objects will be arranged in the order you found them. There are better ways of doing this than using this form. For example, if your records are in the computer, you can generate a list of items in one location and check them off as they are found.

Accession No.	Object	Location	Comment

A-9 LOAN FORM FOR LOANS FROM THE MUSEUM

The loan form should contain this information:

- What is actually being borrowed
- The purpose of the loan
- How the object is to be cared for if particular provisions are required
- Method of transportation and who is responsible for arrangement and payment, with a statement that the museum is responsible only for payment for shipment to the named address
- The conditions under which the object will be displayed
- The exact location at which the object will be
- The exact dates of the loan, wall to wall
- The fair market value of each object
- The type and nature of the insurance and who is responsible for it
- A clause detailing conditions if the loan is terminated early
- A statement about how the conditions of the loan are to be amended
- A statement that the total agreement is contained in the form and attachments, and that no other conditions apply
- Special conditions
- Conditions for protecting intellectual rights and controlling the use of photography
- The name and signature of the responsible parties
- Date of signatures

An example of typical conditions for a loan follows.

CONDITIONS CONCERNING LOANS FROM THE HERO COUNTY HISTORICAL SOCIETY

The Hero County Historical Society lends items from its collections only to museums, historical societies, libraries, other educational organizations, and approved conservators that, according to the Society, can comply with the conditions stated below.

The conditions, as stated on this form, and any attachments, represent the total agreement between the Hero County Historical Society (hereafter "the Society") and the individual, institution, or agency borrowing the object(s) (hereafter "the Borrower"). No other terms are binding on the Society. The objects are loaned for the purposes and the times stated on this form. The form is not valid unless signed by a qualified representative of the Society.

The borrower is required to have an all-risk fine arts insurance policy from an insurance company licensed to do business in the State of Franklin on all objects included on this form, at the value stated, with the Society listed as an additional insured. The Borrower will furnish the Society with a certificate of insurance with a 120-day cancellation clause.

Objects are to be displayed at the place designated and in the manner approved by the Society. All objects listed on this form are in the condition stated. Object(s) loaned will not be exposed to extremes of temperature, strong light, humidity, noxious fumes, etc., and are to be protected from handling by visitors. The Borrower is required to promptly report about damages to the object(s) in this agreement to the Society. The Borrower will not clean, restore, alter, or conserve the object(s) covered by this agreement unless written approval is given by the Society.

The Borrower may take photographs of the object(s) for record purposes. A single photograph may be taken of each object for a one-time publication in a catalog or similar use approved by the Society. The Society is to receive a copy of all photograph(s) taken of the object(s). No other photography or any other form of reproduction or publication is allowed without the written permission of the Society.

The objects will be shipped via the agent and method stated on this form. Packing, crating, and shipping are the responsibility of the borrower under conditions agreed to by both parties.

The Borrower will credit the Society in all labels, publicity, publications, and public releases of information unless otherwise directed.

The Borrower agrees to keep the Society informed in writing of all changes in address and ownership that affect this agreement. The agreement, and the object(s) listed may not be transferred to a third party without the expressed written agreement of the Society. In the event of a change in address and ownership of the Borrower it is the Borrower's obligation to notify the lender within five (5) working days.

This agreement may be terminated by either party thirty (30) days after a written notice has been delivered to the other party. A registered letter is considered adequate notice. The party terminating the agreement is responsible for paying the cost of shipping. The Society agrees to pay only the cost of shipping that does not exceed shipping to the original address.

This agreement may only be amended by written approval of both parties, and such amendments must be attached to this agreement.

A-10 LOAN FORM FOR LOANS TO THE MUSEUM

The criteria for loans to the museum are pretty much the same as loans from, only this time the lender makes conditions the museum must follow. As a practical matter, this form will be used mainly with private lenders. Other museums will insist that you use their form.

- What is actually being borrowed
- Description
- Condition
- The purpose of the loan
- How the object is to be cared for if particular provisions are required
- Method of transportation and who is responsible for arrangement and payment, with a statement that, upon return of the object, the museum is only responsible for payment for shipment to the named address
- The conditions under which the object will be displayed
- The exact location at which the object will be
- The exact dates of the loan, wall to wall
- The fair market value of each object
- The type and nature of the insurance and who is responsible for it
- The name and signature of the responsible parties
- A clause detailing conditions if loan is terminated early
- A statement about how the conditions of the loan are to be amended
- A statement that the total agreement is contained in the form and attachments, and no other conditions apply
- Special conditions
- Conditions for protecting intellectual rights and controlling the use of photography
- A place for signatures of responsible parties
- Date of signatures

An example of typical conditions for a loan follows.

CONDITIONS GOVERNING LOANS TO THE
HERO COUNTY HISTORICAL SOCIETY

The conditions, as stated on this form, and any attachments, represent the total agreement between the Hero County Historical Society (hereafter "the Society") and the individual, institution, or agency lending the object(s) (hereafter "the Lender"). No other terms are binding on the Society. The objects are loaned for the purposes and the times stated on this form. This form is not valid unless signed by a qualified representative of the Society.

The Society will treat the object(s) as if they were a part of the Society's collection. The condition of the object is as stated on this form or attachments.

The Society agrees to compensate the Lender, through the Society's insurance company, for any loss or damage to the object(s) up to the value listed on this form. If the Lender elects to maintain his/her own insurance, he/she must furnish the Society with a certificate of insurance for the value listed with a 120-day cancellation clause from an insurance company licensed to do business in the state of Franklin with the Society named as additional insured.

The term of the loan is as stated. The loan may be terminated by either party thirty (30) days after written notice is delivered to the other party. A registered letter is sufficient notice of termination. The party cancelling the loan will pay for packing and return shipment, but in no case will the Society pay more than the cost of shipment to the address named on this form.

The Society reserves the right to photograph the object for record purposes. Such photographs will be restricted to the files of the Society. A copy of such photographs will be given to the Lender. All other conditions concerning photography and publication appear on the face of this agreement or in attachments.

The Society will credit the Lender in all labels, publicity, and publications unless otherwise directed.

The Lender agrees to keep the Society informed in writing of all changes in address and ownership. In the event of a change in address and ownership the Society agrees to pay only the cost of shipping that does not exceed the cost of shipping to the original address.

If the Lender cannot, or will not, receive his/her objects back within ninety (90) days after the termination of the agreement, the Society reserves the right to exercise a lower standard of care, and/or charge a storage fee, and/or take title to the object(s) in a manner described by law. A registered letter to the Lender's last known address is sufficient notice of the Society's intention to return the object(s) in this agreement.

This agreement may only be amended by written approval of both parties.

A-11 DEPOSIT LOAN FORMS/TEMPORARY CUSTODY AGREEMENTS

Deposit loans, or temporary custody agreements, are very much like any other loan to the museum except:

- The loan is for a shorter time, usually between 30–90 days.
- The museum does not agree to pay for any damage of loss except in the case of gross negligence.
- Pickup and delivery is usually the responsibility of the lender.

Deposit loans are usually used for the following purposes:

- Short-term research
- Consideration for acquisition
- Photography
- A temporary agreement for incoming loans until the formal loan paperwork can be completed

The clause governing the conditions of the loan might read like this:

It is understood that the object(s) listed on this form are left at the museum for temporary deposit and the museum accepts no responsibility for them other than due care. The lender is responsible for pickup and delivery. The condition is as stated on this form.

Some museums add a clause stating what happens to the items if the lender does not pick them up (item becomes museum property if not picked up within a year of notification, items will be disposed of, etc.). This clause is just to help the museum avoid the problems of abandoned property that can occur with any loan.

Receipt No: _____

Temporary Custody Receipt

Hero County Historical Society

This is to acknowledge receipt of the items listed below by the Hero County Historical Society from:

Name: _____	Date: _____
Address: _____
_____
City: _____ State: _____ Zip: _____
Work#: _____ Home#: _____ Fax#: _____ Cell#:_____
Website: _____ Email: _____

The items listed below are left in the custody of the Hero County Historical Society to be considered as:

☐ An unconditional donation. The Museum reserves the right to keep, lend, or otherwise dispose of the donated material.

☐ To be considered for acquisition.

☐ For identification. Does not constitute an authentication; will not include appraisals. Museum reserves the right to photograph.

☐ For other. Please specify_____

Disposition if not accepted for accession:

☐ Source will pick up ☐ Please dispose of or destroy ☐ May be sold to benefit
Hero County Historical Society

This is a temporary loan that shall not exceed a period of 90 days. The agreement expires on: _____

Items and Description

Received by:

_____
(Signature)

_____
(Date)

Received from:

_____
(Signature)

_____
(Date)

A-12 CONDITION REPORT

Most museums won't have a conservator on staff who can technically assess the items and report their condition. So, the form should be tailored for use by the staff. The form should have spots that require a written answer, not a checkmark for the condition description. You need a form for each object. A form should require specific answers for these things:

- Accession number and name of object.
- Catalog description of the object.
- The date the report was completed.
- Who completed the report.
- Whether this form is a routine report or a damage report.
- If damage is reported, the nature of it, and where, when, and how the damage occurred. It should also record who first noticed the damage.
- Any work required.
- Estimated costs (if known).
- Condition of the finish.
- Condition of the structure.
- The condition of materials making up the object.
- The condition of parts, and if there are parts missing.
- If there is a mechanism, does it work? Is it complete?
- How clean is the object?
- Is there any inherent vice?
- A listing of old repairs.
- Any recommendations.

These forms can be generic or they can be tailored for a certain type of material.[1] A sample of a general condition report form is on the next page.

General Condition Report Form

Object ID Number   Date

Evaluation by (Name/Title)

Object Name/Title

Description

Dimensions

Provenance

Previous Treatments or Conservation

Overall Condition (circle one):

Excellent   Good   Fair   Poor

Overall Condition Notes (Please include location and description of damage, attach photos or sketches):

A-13 LOAN REGISTER

Loan registers are like other registers—they need to contain only enough information to help you find the right record. A typical loan register might look like this:

Loan No.	Object	Lender	Date In	Date Out

There is information on numbering loans in chapter 3.

A-14 DEACCESSION FORMS

In chapter 4 I gave you some criteria for generating a "Justification of Deaccession" form for your institution. The example below contains much of that information. This is an example of the type of information you should bring to your collections committee or board to show what something should be deaccessioned and what should happen to it after it leaves the collection.

Hero County Historical Society

DEACCESSION FORM

Object ID # (s)

Description(s):

Provenance:

Reason for Deaccession:

Method of Disposal

Comments:

The item(s) listed above were approved by the Collections Committee and sent to the Board of Trustees. Date_____

Deaccessioning recommendations approved, noted and authorized by the Board of Trustees.

Date_____

Action Initiated By: _____ Title: _____ Date:_____

Object ID(s):

Source:

Means of acquisition: Gift ___   Purchase ___   Exchange ___
Loan ___   Bequest ___   Unknown ___

Restrictions:

The following records have been searched for relevant information (Circle appropriate response):

Accession logs: Yes/No   Database: Yes/No
Accession file: Yes/No   Other:_____
Research File: Yes/No   _____

Additional Comments:

Deaccessioning Criteria
- The item is no longer relevant to the mission of the Museum.
- The item is redundant or is a duplicate and is not necessary for research or study purposes.
- The item is in poor physical condition
- KHS is unable to preserve or store the item in a responsible manner.
- KHS is ordered to return an object to its original and rightful owner by a court of law; KHS determines that another entity is the rightful owner of the object; or KHS determines that the return of the object is in the best interest of the institution.
- Threat to people or other objects

Methods of Disposal
- Transfer to another institution
- Transfer to Educational Collection
- Public sales such as auction
- Witnessed Destruction

NOTE

1. See Southeaster Registrars Association, *Basic Condition Reporting*, 4th ed.—this book provides details on how to create a condition report, sample forms for different material types, and common terms to use in describing damage.

Appendix B
A Registration Manual for a Volunteer-Run Museum

HERO COUNTY HISTORICAL MUSEUM

The purpose of this manual is to create a policy and procedure to ensure that the Hero County Historical Society will have a registration system that will develop a collection, that will serve the purposes of the Museum, that will register the collection properly, that will preserve all the information on each object, and that will be in conformance with the highest standards of the museum profession.

Statement of Purpose or Mission Statement

The statement of purpose (or the mission) of the Hero County Historical Society states:

[The statement of purpose of the historical agency should appear here.]

[The organization may have a charter, a constitution, and bylaws. The portions affecting collections should appear here.]

[If there is a collection management policy statement separate from the statement of purpose, that should appear here. A sample collections management policy statement appears below.]

To direct these aims, the Board of Trustees has adopted the following collection management policy.
[*Example*]

COLLECTION MANAGEMENT POLICY

The Hero County Historical Society will collect only those items related to the purposes of the Museum, for which it has an ultimate use, and that the Museum can properly store, preserve, and protect. There will be a Collections Committee with the responsibility for developing and implementing a set of registration and collections care practices for the Museum. The manual developing this will be the collections policy of the Corporation and will contain the necessary procedures. At the Annual Meeting, the Collections Committee will report for the Board's approval on the state of the collection and on all new accessions, loans, and deaccessions for the year. In pursuance of these policies the collections committee submits this manual to the Board of Trustees.

 Respectfully submitted,
 Collections Committee
 Adopted by the Board of Trustees on _____.

Collections Committee

There will be a Collections Committee composed of at least four members. The Chairperson of this Committee must be a member of the Board, but any member of the Corporation is eligible to serve on the Committee. The Committee will have the general supervision of the collection. The Collections Committee is a standing committee of the Hero County Historical Society.

Curator or Registrar

The Collections Committee, with the approval of the Board, may appoint a Curator and/or a Registrar, who shall be members of the Committee. The Curator will be responsible for the care of the collection, and the Registrar will be responsible for the care of the records of the collection. These members of the Committee will serve an indefinite term at the pleasure of the Board.

Registration File Cabinet

The Committee will acquire a good four-drawer legal-sized fireproof file cabinet with a lock. The cabinet should have an Underwriters seal and a one-hour fire rating. The Committee will place all existing records in that file. It will become the "Registration File Cabinet." The cabinet should be kept locked at all times. The Chairman of the Collections Committee will have a key or the combination, and there will be a copy of the key or combination in the Corporation's safe-deposit box. On the recommendation of the Committee, the Board may assign keys or combinations to other members of the Committee.

Registration and Accession File

The Committee will create an Accession File for each year. All the information on each accession in the year will be in this file. The Committee will create other files on the Registration system as needed. These files will be kept in the Registration File Cabinet.

Acquisition

When a donor offers to donate to the Museum an item or items, the Committee will have him or her sign a Gift Agreement Form. No object may be taken into the Museum unless this form is signed. There shall be three (3) copies of this form: one for the donor, one for the Corporation, and one (the original) for the Committee. All donors should be informed that items are accepted subject to the approval of the Board. The original form should be filed in the Accession File.

In the instance of a purchase, the bill of sale and all other documents will be placed in the Accession File. Before the Treasurer disposes of any cancelled check, those related to the collections should be placed in the proper Accession file.

No member of the Board of Trustees, or the Museum Committee, may evaluate an object offered for gift. Where such evaluations are requested, the Society will confine itself to cooperating with a qualified appraiser, who is retained by the donor.

Accession Register

The Committee will acquire a well-bound record book for the Museum's use as a register. The first one hundred pages should be left blank to record the existing collection. At the beginning of the next page, the Registrar will write the year this manual is adopted _____ and columns for the accession numbers, types of objects, the sources, and the dates of acquisition. If a computer is used for the registration system, then the register will be part of that system.

The Committee will take the items existing in the collection at the time this manual is adopted and try to correlate them with existing records and list them in the Register in the same fashion as the new accessions, and enter them in the front of the Register. The Committee will be sure to record all accessions in the Register including the address of the source of the accession and the date of the acquisition. All entries into the Register will be in indelible ink. The Register is to be kept in the Registration File Cabinet.

Accession Ledger

The Collections Committee will have the Accession Records typed on high-quality archival paper and bound at some convenient interval, say each year. There will be two copies of the Accession Ledger: one will be kept in the Museum library under archival conditions; the other will be the use copy. If the registration system is kept in a computer, the ledger will be part of that system.

Accession Number

The Committee will assign the number one (1) to the first object acquired under the new system, the number two (2) to the second, number three (3) to the third, and so on.

At the beginning of each calendar year, the Committee will start a new page in the Accession Ledger for that year, but the numbers will continue in series.

Only one person will keep the Accession Ledger and assign numbers, and if there is a Registrar, it will be that person. No one may use a number unless the number before has been used. The number shall be placed on the object according to museum standards and the number shall be placed on all documents associated with each accession and those documents filed in the Accession File.

Accession Record

Each object accessioned will have a Worksheet filled in on it. These are to be kept in the Accession File Cabinet until copied and bound into the Accession Ledger.

Catalog Card

The information on each Worksheet will be copied onto a catalog card. These will be filed alphabetically by the title of each object.

Donor File

At the end of each calendar year, the Registrar shall make up a file of donors and other sources. The card file shall contain the donor's or source's name and accession number associated with each name. Only one card shall be made on a donor.

Acknowledgment of Gifts

Each gift to the collection shall be acknowledged by the Collections Committee, either with a Gift Form or by letter, thanking the donor for the gift on behalf of the Corporation. A copy of this form or letter, with the accession number(s) on it, shall be placed in the Accession File. All gifts displayed in the Museum must bear the name(s) of the donor(s) in this fashion, "Gift of XYZ." From time to time, the Committee shall supply the Publications Committee with a list of donors for publication in the Newsletter.

Deaccessioning

It is the policy of the Corporation to deaccession as few items from the collections as possible. From time to time, the Collections Committee may wish to remove items from the collections for the following reasons: the item(s) is/are not germane to the collection; it duplicates a better example; it is a fake or not as represented; its condition threatens itself or the rest of the collection; or the Museum cannot take care of the object properly. On the Committee's recommendation, the Board, with two-thirds of the total membership in attendance approving, may declare an item deaccessioned. The deaccessioned item should be sold at public auction, traded or donated to another educational agency, or destroyed. No deaccession item may be conveyed in any manner to a member of the Board, a member of the Collections Committee, or to anyone holding a post of trust or honor in the Corporation. Funds acquired from deaccessioning must be used to purchase other objects for the collection or to conserve items in the collection.

Loans

Loans to the Museum shall only be for the purpose of enhancing the Museum's exhibits. The lending party will sign the properly executed loan form. The loan will be insured, using the Museum's carrier. The loan will be approved by the Committee and submitted for approval to the Board of Trustees at their next regular meeting.

Loans from the Museum may only be made for the purposes of display in an exhibit which enhances the Corporation's purpose. The borrower will sign a properly executed loan form. The borrower shall furnish proof of insurance or of financial responsibility. Loans from the Museum must be approved in advance by the Board of Trustees.

Objects may not be borrowed or lent for a period of more than one year, but may be renewed from year to year for a total period of three years.

Report to the Board of Trustees

The Collections Committee shall submit a report to the Board of Trustees, at the Annual Meeting, submitting a written report on all new accessions for the year, all outstanding loans, and commenting on the general condition of the collection, a statement of work achieved, and any other matter it deems necessary.

Copy of the Records

At the end of the calendar year, the Committee shall have the records for the year copied. This shall include all documents, pages in the Accession Ledger, and copies of correspondence. The master copy of this shall be kept in [name of a safe place away from the Museum]. Another copy shall become the working record for the Museum.

Protection of Intellectual Assets

For the purposes of this policy, the intellectual assets of the Society consist of the images of objects and documents in the collection, the image of the Museum building, the images and content of programs, physical copies of objects in the collection, and dissimilar devices. When permission is made to photograph, copy, or otherwise use this intellectual property, permission is limited to a one-time use for specific purposes. A blanket, long-term, or unlimited use of intellectual property may not be granted under any circumstances.

Ethics

All actions of the Board should be such that it avoids an apparent as well as an actual conflict of interest with any specific aspect of the Museum operation and its collection. The members of the Board will follow the practices in *Code of Ethics for Museums* (Washington, DC: AAM, 1994).

Amending the Registration Manual

The Collections Committee may suggest amendments to this manual to the Board. Upon approval, these amendments will become part of this manual.

*   *   *

The documents and forms implementing this manual are attached as a reference.

Appendix C

Example of a Museum Collection Policy for a Museum with Professional Staff

**COLLECTIONS MANAGEMENT POLICY
AND MANUAL**

Hero County Historical Society Museum

This document contains the policy and practices governing the Museum collection of the Hero County Historical Society.

This manual was developed by the Museum Committee consisting of the following members:

XXXXXXXXXXXXXXXXXXXX, Chairperson
XXXXXXXXXXXXXXXXXXX
XXXXXXXXXXXXXXXXXXX
XXXXXXXXXXXXXXXXXXX
XXXXXXXXXXXXXXXXXXX
YYYYYYYYYYYYYYYYYYYY, Museum Director, ex officio.
January 26, 20XX

Statement of Purpose

The Statement of Purpose of the Hero County Historical Society as given in the charter which was granted in the Superior Court, County of Hero, the State of Franklin, April 16, 1976, is:

[Example]

"The purpose of the Hero County Historical Society shall be to investigate, elucidate, and publish facts on Hero County history; to preserve objects of historical significance; to receive contributions; and to encourage patriotism and public interest in history."

Subsequently, on the adoption of the new constitution of the Society on June 12, 1977, the Board added the provision that this Society be a nonprofit organization.

In the bylaws adopted on September 30, 1978, this provision provided for a Museum Committee to operate the Museum.

[Example]

"Article XII: The Board may appoint a Museum Director and other staff and set their duties, conditions of work, and compensation. The Museum Director will have the general oversight of the Museum and be responsible for the

Museum building, exhibits, program, and collection, and shall have the direction of the staff. The Director shall be an ex officio member of all committees except the Nominating Committee."

Since the original conception of the Society and Museum did not foresee the present nature of our organization, and since the above clauses in our bylaws, as well as other clauses in our charter and constitution, as well as policies and procedures adopted as resolutions over the course of time, do not provide for a modern museum program, this Collections Manual supersedes all provisions in the constitution and bylaws of the respecting Museum and its collection and become the operating document for the Museum collection.

Collection Management Policy

The collections management policy statement is intended to further define the clauses in the constitution and bylaws respecting the Museum collection.

[Example]

It is the policy of the Hero County Historical Society to collect only those items for the Museum that were made and/or used in Hero County; were associated with a person, place, or event in Hero County; or, to a limited extent, are typical or representative of objects made or used in Hero County; and which are of a historical, cultural, or aesthetic nature, for which the Museum can care for, and which fall in the period of the founding of Hero County.

After complying with the requirements for changes to the constitution and bylaws of the Society, this manual was adopted by the Board of Trustees, Hero County Historical Society, March 26, 20XX.

*   *   *

Responsibility

The Museum Director is responsible for the Museum and is solely responsible for its collection. The Director will work with the Museum Committee to improve the Museum. He or she, with the approval of the Collections Committee, shall have the authority to accept acquisitions for the Museum collection. He or she shall have the sole authority to make or accept loans. The Director will, from time to time, recommend items from the collection that are to be deaccessioned. The Director will report from time to time to the Board on the condition of the collection. The Museum Committee will act as the liaison in collection matters between the Board and the Director.

Computer and Data Security

The Director is responsible for all the collection records. He or she is solely responsible for assigning access to the records of all types. He or she will assign passwords to other staff as needed. The master password shall be kept in the Museum safe. The Director will archive the original copies of the database application program(s) and such other application programs that may be necessary to extract data. The director shall make a backup of the records on a daily basis. One copy of the backup will be kept with the computer and one copy will be kept offsite. A paper backup shall be made and archived every year.

All the registration records will be kept in a locked fireproof file cabinet with at least a one-hour fire rating. The cabinet shall be kept closed except when in use. The Museum Director is responsible for the security of this cabinet and shall have a key or the combination. A duplicate key or copy of the combination will be kept by the Secretary in the Society's safe-deposit box.

Before adopting a new data management program, the Director will assure himself or herself that the data managed by this program is transferable to the new program.

Acquisition and Registration

The acquisition of objects should expand and refine the Museum collection and aid in carrying out the Corporation's purpose. The purpose of registration of the Museum objects is to:

- preserve any associations with historic events, places, or persons than an object may have;
- promote the preservation of the object itself;
- establish the Society's right of title to the object; aid in the interpretation of the object; and
- allow the Society to identify and account for every object in the collection.

Acquisition of an object is after the Director submits copies of a Justification for Accession Form, with a signed Gift Agreement or bill of sale, and any other pertinent document, to the Collection Committee for approval. The Museum will accept no gift in which the Museum's use of the object, or the Museum's right to display or not display the object, is limited in any way, or if the Museum is limited in any way from breaking up collections. However, the Museum may occasionally enter into partial ownership arrangements, life tenures, limited ownerships, or any sharing of title or possession for unique items that will be a significant addition to the collection, but only on the advice of an attorney, and with the expressed approval of the Board.

[A section similar to this may be required if there is an existing collection.]
On adoption of this manual, the Director will take immediate steps to see that every object existing in the collection has:

1. An accurate Accession Record and description
2. A unique record in the Museum database
3. A unique accession number
4. All known documentary information known about the object filed in an accession file and identified by the accession number of the object

[This section is required in all manuals.]
All new objects taken into the collection after the adoption of this manual will have the following:

Paper Records
1. A transfer of title document. In the case of gifts, this is a valid Gift Agreement. In the case of purchases, this is a valid bill of sale. Bequests must have a binding transfer from the estate.
2. A Justification for Accession Form.
3. In the case of gifts, an acknowledgment of gift in the form of a copy of a letter or a form.
4. A unique accession number permanently affixed to the object.
5. An accession file on each accession in a secure file cabinet.
6. Copies of all documents filed in the accession file.

Computer Records
1. A complete record on each object in the Museum database. This record will contain enough data in appropriate fields so that the Museum may easily extract the following information:

a. Management data, or data that relates the object and the records to each other.

b. Descriptive data, or catalog information; data about the object that can mainly be acquired by examining the object itself, or from fairly simple research techniques.

c. Historical data that places the object in a historical context with people, places, or events.

2. The original equipment manufacturers' software for the system software, data management, Museum record keeping and any other pertinent programs.

Every object will have its own record, including sets and objects en suite with other objects.

The Director will acknowledge all gifts by a personal letter or may request that an Acknowledgment of Gift by signed by the President.

Accession Number

Each object will be numbered with a unique accession number. The accession number will have a control number, which will be the year of accession (with the exceptions noted below). The second number will be the accession number. In each year, the first accession will be assigned the number 1 (one), the second 2 (two), and continuing in strict sequence to the last accession of the year. The third number will be the catalog number. The catalog numbers will begin with 1 (one) for the first object in the accession and continue in strict sequential order until all objects in the accession have been numbered. If there is but one object in the accession, it will be given the catalog number 1 (one).

An example would be the accession number 1990.26.3, in which 1990 is the year of accession, 26 is the accession number and the twenty-sixth accession of the year, and 3 is the catalog number and the third object in the accession.

In the case of the existing collection, the accessions that have known provenance are to be registered with this numbering system. All the objects with an unknown provenance existing in the collection at the time of the adoption of this manual are to be given the accession number 1 (one); in 1990 that would be 1990.1.XX, etc.

Nomenclature

The museum will follow the system developed by Robert Chenhall, *Nomenclature 4.0 for Museum Cataloging: Robert G. Chenhall's System for Classifying Cultural Objects* (Lanham, MD: Rowman & Littlefield, 2015), in naming objects and in classifying the catalog. The nomenclature shall be confined to terms actually used in the Museum registration system. The computer registration system should be able to produce a lexicon of the terms used by the Museum.

[The number and types of catalogs will be radically changed if there is a computer. There may not be a catalog per se, but just the ability to generate certain types of records.]

Catalogs

The purpose of the Museum catalog is to give the Museum easy access to the records and collection to aid the Museum staff in accounting. The Museum's registration report should be able to produce the following catalogs, either on-screen or in written reports:

1. All the records by accession number in numerical order.

2. All the objects alphabetically by title.

3. All the objects by source. This report should be able to show the different types of sources (donor, purchase, bequest, etc.).
4. A priority list of conservation needs.
5. All the objects by location.
6. A listing of the value of each object and a total value for the listing.
7. The ability to pull up records by the object's association.
8. Depending on the nature of the Museum's program you may also wish to produce a list of objects on loan *to* the Museum. Under #6 above, the program should already be able to produce a list of objects on loan *from* the museum.
9. The Museum should be able to make "string searches" to extract useful data from the file.

Measurements

All measurements are to be in the inch/foot system. Any computer application program that the Museum acquires must have the ability to convert these to the metric system.

Deaccessioning

The purpose of deaccessioning is to refine the collection so it will help carry out the Society's purpose.

The Museum will only deaccession objects from its collection for the following reasons:

1. Duplication of a better example.
2. The condition of the object threatens itself or the rest of the collection.
3. The object is not germane to the collection.
4. The Museum cannot care for the object properly.
5. The authenticity of the object is questionable.

The Museum will not deaccession objects that have a known history related to our purpose, or that are from living donors, or were accessioned less than twenty-five years previously, unless the object is deteriorated to a point where it threatens itself or the collection or its authenticity is questionable.

Moneys received from deaccessioning may be used only for purchasing new objects for the collection or conserving other objects in the collection.

Using the justification for Deaccessioning Form, the Director will recommend that an object be deaccessioned to the Museum Committee. If approved, the Committee will make a similar recommendation to the Board of Trustees. On its approval, the object will be disposed of and a record of the disposal will be made.

Objects may be disposed of only by a public auction, absolute destruction, or exchange or transfer with another historical agency with a purpose similar to the Society's. No deaccessioned object may be conveyed in any manner to a member of the Board of Trustees, the Museum staff, or anyone holding a post of trust or honor in the Society.

The Museum may exchange or transfer objects in its collection for which it can no longer care or which fit the other criteria of the deaccession process. These transfers or exchanges will be with other museums or educational agencies that can properly care for the object. Any object received in an exchange must fit the Museum's collection policy. Exchanges and transfers must be approved by the Collection Committee and/or Board, as with any other accession or deaccession.

A note that the object has been deaccessioned will be entered on the paper accession record in red ink. Computer records shall be flagged to indicate that the object has been deaccessioned.

Loans

The purpose of loans is to enhance the mission of the Society. Loans from the Museum should extend the Society's purpose outside the walls. Loans to the Museum should augment the Society's purpose while increasing the effectiveness of the collection.

The Director has the sole authority to recommend that the Museum lend or borrow objects. He or she will not lend or borrow objects without a properly executed Loan Form.

The Museum may not accept or grant "permanent loans" or loans for a term longer than three years.

Loans to the Museum

The Museum will borrow items for exhibit only using a properly executed Loan Form. The terms of the loan will be one year. If the exhibit extends past one year, the loan may be extended for a year, on a year-to-year basis, but for no more than three years in total.

Loans to the Museum will be confined to those objects for which the Museum can care for under the same standards as its own collection.

Loans from the Museum

The Museum will lend objects primarily for exhibition in another museum or to a qualified conservator for conservation. Loans from the Museum will be made only on a properly executed Loan Form. Loans may be made to other nonprofit educational agencies if the Director is assured that the object will be cared for and displayed in a manner which meets or exceeds the Museum standards. Loans will be made only to institutions that have a standard of care equaling or exceeding ours.

The term of a loan from the Museum is one year. For extended loans, the period may be extended for a year on a year-to-year basis but for no longer than three years.

[The Museum may wish to adopt a clause such as this if the Museum has a number of permanent loans or unknowns in the collection.]

Permanent Loans and Unknowns

It is the Museum policy to resolve any questions concerning permanent loans and objects with unknown sources as soon as feasible. Immediately after the first inventory of the collection is completed, the Director will prepare a list of permanent loans and objects with unknown sources. The Director will present this list to the Collection Committee with any comments he or she may wish to make. After consideration of this list, the Collection Committee may consult the Museum's attorney and report to the Board any recommendations it may wish to make. The eventual disposition of this class of objects will be made a part of this manual.

Photography of the Collection

The Museum will take a digital image of each object in the collection. These images are intended for identification. They will be cataloged by the accession number of the object. Such number will be clearly visible in each image.

Conservation and Storage

On adoption of this manual, the Director will immediately take steps to prepare a report on the conservation needs of the Museum. The Director will, from time to time, make recommendations to the Board on the conservation of certain objects. The Director will report on the condition of the collection in his or her annual report.

Each record of an object in the Museum registration system will be tagged with a priority number for conservation, where 1 (one) requires the most immediate attention, and 5 (five) requires the least. Objects in the 4 and 5 classification will be considered exhibitable.

Each object will be assigned a permanent location and the object will be said to "live" at that spot. When objects are moved, the new location will be tracked.

Inventory

The Museum will inventory its collection each year. The inventory will consist of an examination of each object and the records. The condition of each object shall be noted. Records will be updated as needed. The inventory list for each year will be filed in the accession file.

[If the Museum insures or places a value on the objects in its collection.]

Evaluations of the Collection

At the time of accession, the Museum will establish a value for each object in the accession. These values will be used to insure the collection and establish a replacement value for loans from the Museum. These values will be updated, if necessary, during the inventory. These values are confidential and are to be revealed only at the discretion of the Director.

Appraisals

No member of the Museum staff, or the Board of Trustees, or of the Museum Committee, may appraise an object as to its monetary value, or give more than a qualified assessment of identity of age for any object that is not the Museum's property. The Museum will not pay an outside appraiser to establish a value on any object being donated to the Museum. In the case of gifts to the Museum, the Museum, when requested, will confine two or more qualified professional appraisers and cooperate with any appraiser the donor selects.

The Director will not evaluate incoming loans but will depend on the owner to supply value. In the case the value is unknown, a suitable appraiser shall be retained.

Properties

The expendable non-collection property of the Museum or the Society is not part of this policy or manual. It should be accounted for in a manner recommended by our auditor. Reproductions of authentic objects used in exhibits or demonstrations are properties and should not be accessioned. In the event a property is taken into the collection, it shall be accessioned in the regular manner and given the same care as any other item in the collection.

Ethics

All actions of the Board and the Museum staff should be such that they avoid an apparent as well as an actual conflict of interest with any aspect of the Museum operation and its collection. The members of the Board and the Museum staff will follow the practices in the Ethics Policy adopted by the Board, [Date]. In cases not covered by the Museum Ethics Policy, the Corporation will follow the American Alliance of Museums, *Code of Ethics for Museums*.

Protection of Intellectual Assets

For the purposes of this policy, the intellectual assets of the Society consist of the images of objects and documents in the collection, the image of the Museum building, the images and content of programs, and physical copies of objects in the collection. When permission is made to photograph, copy, or otherwise use this intellectual property, permission is limited to one-time use for specific purposes. A blanket, long-term, or unlimited use of intellectual property may not be granted under any circumstances.

Access

The Museum will grant qualified researchers with legitimate research goals in mind equal access to the collections on a bona fide need-to-know basis. The Director establishes what the qualifications of the researcher and the legitimate goals are. Moreover, the Director may limit access to the object to specified methods of examination and to certain times. The Director may require a written request, stating which objects are to be examined, the method of examination, and the reasons for the examination.

The Museum registration records are not a public record but should be considered confidential information. The Director may provide portions of the registration records to qualified researchers but restrict access to donor, location, and value.

Other Types of Collections

[This manual does not cover such items as books, manuscripts, anthropological specimens, and so on, which have well-recognized methods of registration. If the Museum has a large enough collection in these other areas, provisions for their care should be incorporated in this manual.]

Public Document

This policy is a public document. A copy shall be kept in the Museum office and made available to any interested person.

Amendments

This Collections Policy and Manual may be amended by a resolution of the Board of Trustees following provision in the constitution and bylaws respecting amendments.

*   *   *

The documents and forms implementing this manual are attached as a reference.

Bibliography

Note: The American Alliance of Museums (formerly American Association of Museums) will be referred to as AAM. The American Association for State and Local History will be referred to as AASLH.

AAM. *Peer Review Manual.* Washington, DC: American Association of Museums, 2005.

AAM Registrars Committee, Professional Practices Subcommittee. "Loan Survey Report." May 1990.

AAM Registrars Committee. *General Facilities Report.* Washington, DC: American Association of Museums, 2008.

Alten, Helen. "Materials for Labeling Collections." *The Upper Midwest Museums Collections Care Network* 1, no. 6 (Winter 1996), 1–7.

Association of Registrars and Collections Specialists. *Old Loan Abandoned Property Disposition.* https://www.arcsinfo.org/ programs/resources/legislation/old-loan-abandoned-property-disposition. 2013. Accessed on December 18, 2016.

Baca, Murtha, Patricia Harping, Elisa Lanzi, Linda McRae, and Ann Whiteside. *Cataloging Cultural Objects: A Guide to Describing Cultural Objects and Their Images.* Chicago: American Library Association, 2006.

Blackaby, James R., Chair, Common Data Bases Task Force. "Final Report to the Field, September 1989." *Common Agenda for History Museums.* Nashville: AASLH, 1989.

Blackaby, James R., Chair, Common Data Bases Task Force. "Managing Historic Data: Report of the Common Agenda Task Force." *Special Report #3.* Nashville: AASLH, 1989.

Bourchier, Paul, Heather Dunn, and the Nomenclature Task Force. *Nomenclature 4.0 for Museum Cataloging.* Lanham, MD: Rowman & Littlefield/AASLH, 2015.

Buck, Rebecca A., and Jean Allman Gilmore. *Collection Conundrums.* Washington, DC: American Association of Museums, 2007.

Buck, Rebecca A., and Jean Allman Gilmore, eds. *Museum Registration Methods, Fifth Edition.* Washington, DC: AAM Press, 2010.

Carwell, Clarissa, and Rebecca Buck. "Acquisition and Accessioning." In Buck and Gilmore, *Museum Registration Methods, Fifth Edition,* 44–57.

Case, Mary, ed. *Registrars on Record: Essays on Museum Collections Management.* Registrars Committee. Washington, DC: AAM, 1988.

DeAngelis, Ildiko. "Old Loans." In Buck and Gilmore, *Museum Registration Methods, Fifth Edition*, 2010, 85–90.

Duggan, Anthony J., Section Editor. "Collection Management." In Thompson et al., *Manual of Curatorship*, 113–376.

Fahy, Anne, ed. *Collections Management*. Leicester Readers in Museum Studies. New York: Routledge, 1995.

Feldman, Franklin, Stephen E. Weil, and Susan D. Beiderman. *Art Law: Rights and Liabilities of Creators and Collectors*. 2 volumes. Boston: Little, Brown, 1986.

Fishman-Armstrong, Susan E., and Deborah Rose Van Horn, "Considerations for Implementing a Bar Code System in a Museum." *Collections* 4, no. 4 (Fall 2008), 333–348.

Freitag, Sally, and Cherie Summers, and Judy Cline. "Loans," In Buck and Gilmore, *Museum Registration Methods, Fifth Edition*, 120–132.

Guthe, Carl E. *So You Want a Good Museum? A Guide to the Management of Small Museums*. Washington, DC: AAM, 1957.

Hankins, Scott. "Photography." In Buck and Gilmore, *Museum Registration Methods, Fifth Edition*, 277–285.

IMLS. "A Framework of Guidance for Building Good Digital Collections." November 6, 2001.

Johnston, Tamara, Robin Meador-Woodruff, and Terry Segal. "Collections Management: Marking." In Buck and Gilmore, *Museum Registration Methods, Fifth Edition*, 233–276.

Keown, C. Timothy, Amanda Murphy, and Jennifer Schansberg. "Ethical and Legal Issues: Complying with NAGPRA." In Buck and Gilmore, *Museum Registration Methods, Fifth Edition*, 448–457.

Koelling, Jill Marie, *Digital Imaging: A Practical Approach*. Walnut Creek, CA: AltaMira Press, 2004.

Lanzi, Elisa, et al. *Introduction to Vocabularies: Enhancing Access to Cultural Heritage Information*. Los Angeles: J. Paul Getty Trust, 1998.

Lewis, Geoffrey D. "Collections, Collectors and Museums: A Brief World Survey." In Thompson et al., *Manual of Curatorship*, 7–22.

Lewis, Ralph H. *Manual for Museums*. Washington, DC: National Park Service, 1979.

Light, Richard, et al. *Museum Documentation Systems: Developments and Applications*. London: Butterworths, 1986.

Longstreth-Brown, Kitty, and Rebecca Buck. "Records Management: Manual Systems." In Buck and Gilmore, *Museum Registration Methods, Fifth Edition*, 155–160.

Malaro, Marie C., and Ildiko Pogany DeAngelis. *A Legal Primer on Managing Museum Collections, Third Edition*. Washington, DC: Smithsonian Books, 2012.

Malaro, Marie C. *Museum Governance: Mission, Ethics, Policy*. Washington, DC: Smithsonian Institution Press, 1994.

Manning, Anita. "Converting Loans to Gifts." *AASLH Technical Leaflet #94*. Nashville: AASLH, 1977.

McCormick, Maureen. "Inventory." Steiner, Christine. "Copyright." In Buck and Gilmore, *Museum Registration Methods, Fifth Edition*, 300–306.

Morris, Martha and Antonia Moser. "The Basics: Deaccessioning." In Buck and Gilmore, *Museum Registration Methods, Fifth Edition*, 100–107.

Museum Documentation Association. *Practical Museum Documentation, Second Edition*. Duxford, Cambridgeshire, UK: Museum Documentation Association, 1981.

O'Connel, Brian. *The Board Member's Book: Making a Difference in Voluntary Organizations.* N.P.: Foundation Center, 1985.

Orlowski, Thomas J. *Smart Selection and Management of Association Computer Systems.* Washington, DC: American Society of Association Directors, 1985.

Pearsall, Margot P., and Holly B. Uselth. "Registration Records in a History Museum." In Dudley and Wilkinson, *Museum Registration Methods,* 245–266. Washington, DC: AAM, 1979.

Perry, Kenneth D. *The Museum Forms Book, Third Edition.* Austin: Texas Association of Museums and Mountain-Plains Museum Association, 2000.

Peterson, Toni, Director. *Art and Architectural Thesaurus.* New York: Oxford University Press, 1994.

Phelan, Marilyn. *Museum Law: A Guide for Officers, Directors, and Counsel, Fourth Edition.* Lanham, MD: Rowman & Littlefield, 2014.

Phelan, Marilyn. *Museums and the Law.* Nashville: AASLH, 1982.

Porter, Daniel R., III. "Current Thoughts on Collections Policy: Producing the Essential Document for Managing Your Collections." *Technical Report 1.* Nashville: AASLH, 1985.

Porter, Daniel R., III. "Developing a Collections Management Manual." *Technical Report 7.* Nashville: AASLH, 1987.

Quigley, Suzanne, and Perian Sully. "Records Management: Computerized Systems." In Buck and Gilmore, *Museum Registration Methods, Fifth Edition,* 161–183.

Racz, Gabor R. "Improving Collection Maintenance through Innovation: Bar-Code Labeling to Track Specimens in the Processing Stream." *Collections* 1, no. 3 (February 2005), 227–241.

Registrars Committee–American Alliance of Museums. *U.S. Old Loan Legislation by State.* 2013. http://www.rcaam.org/cms/wp-content/uploads/2011/06/Museum-Property-Disposal-Legislation-updated-July-20132.doc. Accessed on December 18, 2016.

Reibel, Daniel B. "Classification Systems and the Size of the Registration Systems." ALHFAM *Proceedings* 27 (2005), 160–161.

Rivard, Paul E., and Stephen Miller. "Cataloging Collections-Erratic Starts and Eventual Success: A Case Study." In Fahy, *Collections Management,* 211–214.

Roberts, D. Andrew. "The Development of Computer-Based Documentation." In Thompson et al., *Manual of Curatorship,* 136–141.

Shapiro, Michael S., Brett I. Miller, and Christine Steiner, eds. *A Museum Guide to Copyright and Trademark by the American Association of Museums.* Washington, DC: AAM, 1999.

Shapiro, Michael S., Brett I. Miller, Christine Steiner, and Nicholas D. Ward. *Copyright in Museum Collections.* Washington, DC: AAM, 1999.

Simmons, John. "Managing Things: Crafting a Collections Policy." *Museum News* 83, no. 1 (January/February 2004), 28–31.

Society of American Archivists. *Abandoned Property Project.* http://www2.archivists.org/groups/acquisitions-appraisal-section/abandoned-property-project. Accessed December 18, 2016.

Speckart, Kathryn. "Old Loans: State Legislation." In Buck and Gilmore, *Museum Registration Methods, Fifth Edition,* 91–96.

Steiner, Christine. "Copyright." In Buck and Gilmore, *Museum Registration Methods, Fifth Edition,* 427–435.

Stephenson, Christie, and Patricia McClung, eds. *Delivering Digital Images: Cultural Heritage Resources for Education.* Museum Site Licensing Project, Volume 1. Los Angeles: Getty Information Institute, 1998.

Stone, Sheila M. "Documenting Collections." In Thompson et al., *Manual of Curatorship*, 127–135.

Thompson, John M. A., et al., eds. *Manual of Curatorship: A Guide to Museum Practice.* London: Butterworths, 1984.

Tompkins, William G. "Should Museums Capitalize Their Collections? Or How Much Collateral Is That Caravaggio?" *Museum News* 83, no. 1 (January/February 2004), 27.

Ullberg, Allen, and Patricia Ullberg. *Museum Trusteeship.* Washington, DC: AAM, 1981.

Ullberg, Patricia. "What Happened in Greenville: The Need for Codes of Ethics." *Museum News* 60, no. 2 (November–December 1981), 26–29.

Van Horn, Deborah Rose, Heather Culligan, and Corinne Midgett, eds. *Basic Condition Reporting, Fourth Edition.* Lanham: Rowman & Littlefield, 2015.

Weil, Stephen E. *Beauty and the Beasts: Museums, Art, the Law, and the Market.* Washington, DC: Smithsonian Institution Press, 1983.

Weil, Stephen E., ed. *A Deaccession Reader.* Washington, DC: AAM, 1997.

Weisz, Jackie, Compiler, and Rozana Adams, Series Editor. *Codes of Ethics and Practice of Interest to Museums.* Washington, DC: AAM, 2000.

Williams, Stephen L. "Critical Concepts Concerning Non-Living Collections." *Collections* 1 (2004), 37–66.

Zwiesler, Catherine. "Barcoding." *Spectra* 23, no. 1 (Fall 1995), 18–20.

See also www.AASLH.org/Bookshelf for up-to-date information on collection related information.

Index

About the Authors

Daniel B. Reibel worked in the museum field for over fifty years as a curator or director. His career began at the Detroit Historical Museum, and he went on to work at the Allen County–Fort Wayne Historical Society and the Old Barracks Museum, giving him his experience with small museums. He had a twenty-five-year career with the Pennsylvania Historical and Museum Commission as director of Old Economy Village, the Landis Valley Museum, and Washington Crossing Historic Park and as a regional director. He completed his career in museums as a volunteer in the collections department of the Mercer Museum, Bucks County Historical Society.

Reibel also worked as an on-site visitor for the MAP program, the Accreditation Commission of the American Alliance of Museums, and the American Association for State and Local History. He has held offices in several museum associations.

Deborah Rose Van Horn has worked in the museum field for almost twenty years. Deborah started as a volunteer in small museums before embarking on a career in the museum field. She has spent the last fourteen years at the Kentucky Historical Society, first as the assistant registrar and then as the registrar. Prior to that, she worked at the Lubbock Lake Landmark, the Museum of Texas Tech University, and the Georgia Museum of Natural History.

Deborah is currently the chair of the Southeastern Registrars Association, and she has also served on the board for the Registrars Committee of the American Alliance of Museums as the southeastern representative. She also works with the Southeastern Museums Conference as the co-coordinator for Professional Networks and Affinity Groups.